IN THE NAME OF

ALLAH

THE MOST BENEFICENT, THE MOST MERCIFUL

The Forbidden Relationship
A Handbook on Love, Lust &
Heartbreaks

- **TITLE:** The Forbidden Relationship: A Handbook on Love, Lust & Heartbreaks
- **AUTHOR:** Maryam Yousaf
- **EDITOR:** Umm Marwan Ibrahim
- **ENGLISH EDITION I**

THE FORBIDDEN RELATIONSHIP

A HANDBOOK ON
LOVE, LUST & HEARTBREAKS

MARYAM YOUSAF

Muslima Today

ISBN 978-0-9934078-4-0

Muslima Today

www.muslimatoday.com

Table of Contents

Dedication

I dedicate this book to every Muslim that is being tempted to enter into a forbidden relationship, to the ones already involved in it, to those struggling to get out of it, and even to those that are simply confused with it all.

This book is dedicated to all the innocent souls that have been head-hunted by players; to every heart that has been broken, with countless false desires awoken; to boys and girls, and women and men; to the future sons and daughters, and the youth of tomorrow.

I dedicate this book to those who believe in fairy-tales and love before marriage.

I dedicate this book to everyone who seeks to find the truth about love, lust and heartbreaks.

Author's Note

Praise be to Allah Who has enabled me to write this book – the book I once wished existed. Since long ago, I have wanted to come across a book that illustrates the dangers of *haraam* relationships. A book that offers deep insight into what a *haraam* relationship is and why it is deemed wrong, all the while providing practical steps on how to avoid such relationships, and if worse comes to worst, how to deal with the aftermath of such a relationship.

We find far too many Muslims in the world today who are involved in this dangerous sin. Perhaps it is so because it isn't truly acknowledged as a sin, and is instead desensitised and normalised in our communities. While it is the youth that is most vulnerable to this plague, many youngsters that *do* abstain from getting involved in forbidden relationships do so merely fearing their respective cultural norms. But what they fail to do is realise the Divine Source of this taboo and appreciate the wisdom behind its prohibition. Most youngsters stay oblivious to the detrimental effects that *haraam* relationships have on a person's physical health, mental well-being and the fate of their very soul in this life as well the *aakhirah*.

It is no wonder then why I longed to lay eyes upon a book that would act as a safety net for my Muslim brothers and sisters from falling into this trap. A book that would not only convey the severity of this sin, but go over and beyond in making them think a hundred times about it when tempted. When my pursuit for such a book was in vain, I considered the onus to be on me and decided to write one myself.

This book that you hold in your hands isn't just a manual of do's and don'ts. Rather, it is a handbook that seeks to serve as enlightenment for those who are content in their forbidden relationships, a counsel for those who may be emotionally trapped in them, and a guide for those that wish to break free without being left broken themselves. It is for those who have experienced tragic breakups and now wonder how to piece together their broken hearts. Finally, this book also intends to be a means of glad tidings for those who, by the Mercy of Allah, have been protected from this evil.

I pray that this book gives you, dear reader, the answers to all the questions you have been searching for, and the facts that you need in order to educate, safeguard, and recover yourself from *haraam* relationships.

I urge you to share this book with your friends and family, and to make all those around you aware of it. You never know, by doing so, you may just save someone's heart and soul.

Note to the reader: Although it seems as though I've exclusively addressed the ladies in many places in the book (in part because I have been approached by them most), my advices and admonitions stand true to the menfolk as well.

May Allah make this a source of *sadaqah jaariyah* for me and you.

Aameen.

Maryam Yousaf

Perfect Prince

The perfect prince you want to find

From frog to frog, your heart will pine

No value for yourself, your body or mind

Like a carcass from place to place you will find

Meaningless relationships; your role you can't define

A girlfriend, a mistress, a pastime

The respect of a wife you won't find

If you want happiness, love and value in this lifetime

Then expect to change and live according to the Law of
Allah the Divine

He has raised your status as daughter, sister, and mother to
mankind

Accept His Will and bliss is what you will find

CHAPTER 1

THE *HARAAM* RELATIONSHIP

Simply put, a *haraam* relationship is a relationship in which one is romantically involved with another outside of marriage. It is what we call in casual terms, a 'fling', 'romance', or 'love affair'. There are numerous instances in the Qur'an and Sunnah that explicitly condemn pre-marital relationships. Having a boyfriend or a girlfriend is a serious sin and something that is strictly forbidden in Islam.

Love: *Halaal or Haraam*

Having said that we're disallowed to have lovers before marriage in Islam, the question that may surface in your mind now is this: Is it *haraam* to even have feelings for someone, to love someone? The answer to that is simply 'no'.

It is not *haraam* to like someone or to experience love towards a person and to want to marry them. Love is a feeling that is out of our control. It is something that springs into our hearts without much conscious effort. Just like all other feelings, love is an emotion that overtakes our hearts instinctively. However, if this feeling is the consequence of and/or leads to free mixing, not lowering one's gaze, or getting involved in private conversations, then in such cases

4

it is considered forbidden – *haraam*. In other words, if this emotion of love happens to appear in one's heart but he/she *doesn't* act on it, then there is no blame on him/her. There is nothing wrong with love that grounds itself within the Laws of Allah.

"If love develops for a reason that is not *haraam*, a person cannot be blamed for that, such as one who loves his wife or his slave woman, then he leaves her but that love remains and does not leave him. He is not to be blamed for that. The same applies if he glances accidentally then looks away, but love may settle in his heart without him wanting it to. But he has to ward it off and look away".

(Narrated by Ibn Al-Qayyim in Rawdat al-Muhibbeen, p. 147)

"A person may hear that a woman is of good character and virtuous and knowledgeable, so he may want to marry her. Or a woman may hear that a man is of good character and virtuous and knowledgeable and religiously committed, so she may want to marry him. But contact between the two who admire one another in ways that are not Islamically acceptable is the problem, which leads to disastrous consequences. In this case, it is not permissible for the man to get in touch with the woman or for the woman to get in touch with the man, and say that he wants to marry her. Rather he should tell her *wali* (guardian) that he wants to marry her, or she should tell her *wali* that she wants to marry him, as 'Umar (may Allah be pleased with him) did when he offered his daughter Hafsah in marriage to Abu Bakr and Uthmaan (may Allah be pleased with them both). But if the woman contacts the man directly, this is what leads to *fitnah* (temptation)."

(Liqaa'aat al-Baab il Maftooh)

We realise that Islam does not crush the emotion of love; rather it acknowledges, accepts and nurtures it in the best manner possible. The healthy alternative that Islam provides for lovers is the marriage contract. Every other institution besides marriage would be a means of destruction, and would reap more harm than benefits.

The Prophet (peace be upon him) said: "There is nothing like marriage, for two who love one another."

(Ibn Maajah, Book 9, Hadith 1920; graded 'sound' by Al-Albani)

What Baby Steps Can Lead To

In order to understand the reality of *haraam* relationships, we need to first study the psychology behind people engaging in it. After all, why would anyone gravitate towards a relationship that is actually deemed forbidden in their *deen*?

People in general tend to take emotional relationships intensely. And when their need for emotional relationships with human beings, begin to outweigh the spiritual relationship with their Lord, it leads them to overstep limits set in the religion and transgress into sin.

The Prophet (peace be upon him) saw a young man looking at a young woman, and he turned his head to make him look away, he then said: "I saw a young man and a young woman, and I did not trust the Shaytaan not to tempt them".

(Tirmidhi, Hadith 885; graded 'sound' by Al-Albani)

No one really jumps into a *haraam* relationship at the get-go. It takes a small sin to lead to a bigger one. This is why the Prophet (peace be upon him) averted the man's gaze, so that something as simple as a mere sight does not lead to a sin as grave as fornication. In fact, what we consider to be something very minor can lead to major sins. Therefore, it's important to not take looking at and interacting with the opposite gender – especially when it is not necessary – so lightly. Many of us may think that we know our limits, but unfortunately many of us are not aware of how easily we can lose control and how one thing can lead to another. There are always those baby steps that lead to bigger ones, and when we lose control of our emotions then it's much easier to be tempted and fall into the pit of darkness and sin. Before we know it, we can start to develop feelings for the opposite gender which can seriously cloud our judgement, and soon we find ourselves making excuses as to why it's okay to do what we are doing.

It would be befitting to take into account the famous story of Barsisa. A pious devotee of Allah who went from being immersed in the worship of Allah twenty-four seven, to having an affair with a lady, to committing murder and finally, *shirk* itself!

No one who knew Barsisa to be the pious man that he was would in a million years have imagined this fate for him. And yet, such was his fate – all because of those baby steps. *(Ibn al-Jauzi, Talbees Iblees)*

For more information I highly recommend you to watch the YouTube video *'The Story of Barsisa – The Tricks of Shaytaan'* by Brother Mohamed Hoblos.

The Harm and Dangers of *Haraam* Relationships

There is a great deal of harm that comes from a *haraam* relationship. It surely is a dangerous sin. The effects of a *haraam* relationship can be long-term, and may even last for decades after the relationship ends, and in some cases, for life.

A relationship that is founded on uncertainty, reckless fun and imprudence has detrimental effects on a person's emotional, physical, mental and spiritual well-being. A *haraam* relationship is akin to a disease that plagues everyone, young and old. It has the innate ability to break hearts, not just of the two people involved but of their families too.

They lead to lies, betrayal, secrecy, indecency, wasted time, confusion, guilt, insecurity, weakness, instability, tragedy, heartbreak, suicidal thoughts, depression, deceit, sexually transmitted diseases, and even the murdering of innocent children in the name of 'abortion' – a mouthful of evil. All of this causes nothing but emotional turmoil. It can have a negative impact on future relationships and leave behind nothing but regret, and a deadly attachment that poisons one's insides.

A person could be the most content individual that you would've seen, but the moment they partake in such a sin, they would not only be robbed of their peace, but would also have their faith and worship tarnished.

So please remember dear brothers and sisters: there is always harm in *haraam*.

Chapter 2

AN ISLAMIC INSIGHT

"But perhaps you hate a thing and it is good for you; and perhaps you love a thing and it is bad for you. And Allah knows, while you know not."
(Qur'an, 2:216)

As Muslims who believe in the tenets of Islam, we must always refer to the Divine Source of knowledge – the Word of the Lord of all creation. The problems in our lives arise when we fail to realise that Allah alone knows us and our capabilities better than our own selves. As our Creator, He is the One who is best aware of the human nature, its soul and its body. He alone knows what is best for each of us. And this is why it is crucial that we try our utmost best to abide by His laws.

In the previous section, we briefly touched upon how a *haraam* relationship could be the reason for one's life on earth turning into hell. In this section, we will explore how it could also be the reason for one to enter Hell in the hereafter too. May Allah protect us all.

Shirk and Murder

A mere glance at the numerous Qur'anic verses and Prophetic traditions on the topic of forbidden relationships would give us an idea of the severity of this sin in Islam.

10

"And those who invoke not any other ilaah (god) along with Allah, nor kill such person as Allah has forbidden, except for just cause, nor commit illegal sexual intercourse (zina) and whoever does this shall receive the punishment. The torment will be doubled to him on the Day of Resurrection, and he will abide therein in disgrace. Except those who repent and believe (in Islamic Monotheism), and do righteous deeds"

(Qur'an, 25:68-70)

In this verse, Allah mentions fornication/adultery (*zina*) right beside *shirk* and murder – the most heinous crimes committed against the Creator and His creation, respectively. And the recompense mentioned for it is an eternity in Hell with doubled torment and disgrace.

'Don't Go Near It'

One may wonder, 'an illegal sexual relationship with another can be accepted to be forbidden, but why would a harmless romantic relationship that isn't physical be considered forbidden too?'

Allah answers this question in His Book, saying:

"And come not near to unlawful sex. Verily, it is a faahishah (anything that transgresses its limits: a great sin), and an evil way"

(Qur'an, 17:32)

Allah admonishes man to go nowhere near unlawful sex. He doesn't simply prohibit us from engaging in fornication, but

11

orders to stay away from anything and everything that would lead to it.

Zina (adultery/fornication) isn't just about penetration. There is *zina* of the hand, which is the touch that is forbidden; the *zina* of the eyes is looking at that which is forbidden; while the *zina* of the private parts is the unlawful sexual interaction itself. Recall the 'baby steps' from the previous section here. Allah demands us to cut off any links that could possibly lead to adultery itself.

The Prophet (peace be upon him) said, "Allah has decreed for every son of Adam his share of *zina*, which he will inevitably commit. The *zina* of the eyes is looking, the *zina* of the tongue is speaking, one may wish and desire and the private parts confirm that or deny it".

(Bukhari, Hadith 5889; authentic; Muslim, Hadith 2657; authentic)

Sexual Relationships before Marriage

Having sexual relationships before marriage is known as fornication and is a major sin in Islam. It is amongst one of the worst sins that a Muslim may commit.

Even though the vast majority of Muslims know that it is *haraam,* many still partake in this dreadful sin. They let emotions and the attachment to one another cloud their minds, becoming slaves to their desires. When a person starts mingling with the opposite gender, talking, flirting, and befriending them they may eventually develop feelings for them. Although they may set boundaries and have a relationship with no physical contact in the initial stages, there is no guarantee to these boundaries staying intact. Gazes turn into talks, chats turn into holding hands, to hugs, to kisses and the closer the couple gets, the more physical they will end up. This is why even the holding of hands is a serious matter in Islam.

"For one of you to be stabbed in the head with an iron needle is better for him than that he should touch a woman who is not permissible for him".

(At-Tabaraani in al-Kabeer, Hadith 486; graded 'authentic' by Al-Albani)

Men – especially those in relationships – tend to be impatient. They could be even more so if they are engaged. One such fellow may say to his would-be, 'We are going to get married anyway so there's no problem in getting intimate now', or 'You are my wife already' – even though she really isn't yet – and other such sugar-coated statements only to play on her weaknesses and soften her heart so that she gives into him and his requests easily.

Dear sisters, realise that just because a man addresses you as his wife, it does not *make* you his wife. Men are very much capable of using their charm to get what they want. Think of the couples that were engaged or in serious relationships once but are no longer together. They may have had endless conversations about being happily married, detailed discussions about the number of kids they were going to have and may have even picked their names. But at the end of it all when things didn't work out, one question arises: Did all that time spent together, all those efforts put into the relationship, and the constant talks of the future mean anything at all? It is safe to say 'no' because ultimately, it was all just baseless talk and broken promises. So beware of such negligence, and don't get carried away with sweet-talk; they mean nothing without having a *nikkah* (marriage).

Unfortunately, people commit *zina* assuming that they will ultimately get married to the other. But even if the couple do *eventually* get married, the fact is that as a *non-mahram*, even one's fiancé is unlawful for them until after the marriage has taken place. Why, you are not allowed to even touch one another. It is *haraam* and a major sin to have sexual relations with a person before marriage even if you are engaged to them. It is still unacceptable, and isn't justifiable one bit.

This sin is so serious that the greatest blessing of all which is *eeman* (faith) is removed from the fornicator until the evil act is finished. The Prophet (peace and blessings be upon him) said:

"Faith comes out of a person whilst he commits fornication."

(Abu Dawud, Book 42, Hadith 95; graded 'authentic' by Al-Albani)

"A fornicator who fornicates is not a believer as long as he commits fornication, and no one who steals is a believer as long as he commits theft, and no one who drinks wine is a believer as long as he drinks it, and repentance may be accepted after that."

(Muslim, Book 1, Hadith 114; authentic)

14

On the flip side, let's take a look at the following *hadith*:

"One of the seven people who will be under the protection of the shade of the throne of Allah on the day of judgment when there will be no shade will be the young man (or woman) who was approached by a respectable beautiful woman but he replied 'I fear Allah'."

(Bukhari, Book 1, Hadith 659; authentic)

Subhanallah (Glory be to Allah), how blessed is it to have the shade of Allah's Throne just because you restrained yourself, and you rejected someone out of the fear of Allah. I advise you to remind yourself of this narration whenever you feel tempted.

Extra Marital Affairs

Allah says:

"Tell the believing men to lower their gaze (from looking at forbidden things), and protect their private parts (from illegal sexual acts)".

(Qur'an, 24:30)

When one does not lower their gaze, they start to feel ungrateful for all the blessings that Allah has bestowed on them. All of a sudden, one's wife – the very woman that the man is married to, doesn't seem beautiful enough for him, and vice versa with the women.

What such spouses don't stop to think is that the women that seem to be perpetually dressed-up, the men that are constantly in designer clothes, and people that generally look as if they've just stepped out of a catwalk with everything perfectly put together, actually spend hours upon hours in trying to appear 'perfect'. So much of their money and time goes in to getting that 'desirable' look, that none of it is truly real. Such people appear even more perfect on their social media with all the editing and filtering that goes into that one picture-perfect photo that they finally settled on after twenty-something snaps. Whilst the overwhelmed wife at home is probably too caught up looking after her husband, her children, the household, and maybe even holding down a job to have any time at all for herself. And that loyal husband perhaps spends all his money on taking care of his wife and children, the house, and the monthly bills, leaving little money left for him to spend on himself.

Dear reader, realise that looking at men and women other than our spouses and desiring them won't solve our problems in any way; such an attitude is only the start of our destruction whilst our eyes and, sooner or later, hands begin to wander in the wrong direction. May Allah protect us.

Why don't you, o' husband, do what you can and give your wife the time and opportunity that she needs in order to make herself look exactly the way you would like her to? Gift her perfume, a makeup set, or the jewels that you imagine would look good on the woman you love. Why don't you help her more with the house chores, get a babysitter and take her on those romantic dinner dates? But if you don't have the means to do so, at least lower your gaze and stop comparing your wife to someone else's.

And why don't you, dear wife, tell him exactly what you would like instead of beating around the bush? Prepare his favourite meal. Dress up for him. Appreciate him for all of his toils for the family. Verbalise your gratitude for having him as your husband. Praise him in front of his family members. And pamper him so that he doesn't seek for such treatment elsewhere.

Dear couple, always be honest with one another, and don't let any third person wedge themselves into your marriage. You may feel as though someone else is a better listener or that they understand you better than your own spouse. But this isn't the case. You just need to be courageous enough to be honest about your feelings, and work as a married couple together in devising ways to improve your relationship. Don't give up on your marriage – *especially* not for someone that knows you are married yet continues to see you. Stop dishonouring yourself that way and instead ask yourself: 'How do I know for sure that they won't cheat on *me* tomorrow?' Because if they have cheated with you now, then there's no saying that they won't do the same in the future *to* you.

I advise you, brother/sister to not even consider having an affair. Not only will it destroy your own life, but also the lives of all those around you – your spouse's, your children's, your parents' and siblings'. And soon its ruins will spread to the society you live in as well.

And if that is not enough, having an affair is a betrayal of the rights of Allah and a betrayal of the rights of your spouse.

Imam Ahmad (may Allah have mercy on him) said: I do not know of any sin after murder that is worse than *zina*, and he quoted as evidence the hadeeth of 'Abd-Allah ibn Mas'ood who said:

"O Messenger of Allah, which sin is the worst?" He said, "Setting up a rival to Allah when He is the One Who created you." ('Abd-Allah) said: "Then what?" He said, "Killing your child for fear that he may eat with you." ('Abd-Allah) said, "Then what?" He said, "Committing adultery with your neighbour's wife." And confirmation of that was revealed in the Qur'an:

"And those who invoke not any other ilaah (god) along with Allah, nor kill such person as Allah has forbidden, except for just cause, nor commit illegal sexual intercourse and whoever does this shall receive the punishment"

(Qur'an, 25:68)"

(Bukhari, Book 47, Hadith 3484; authentic)

The truth is that all of these false desires are from none other than the Shaytaan. He works night and day to drive you apart. Don't let him win. Dodge his first arrow by lowering your gaze. Then concentrate on finding ways to get your marriage back on track. Communicate and make plans. Do not give up.

The Messenger of Allah (peace be upon him) said, "Verily, Satan places his throne over the water and he sends out his troops. The closest to him in rank are the greatest at causing tribulations. One of them says: I have done this and this. Satan says: You have done nothing. Another one says: I did not leave this man alone until I separated him from his wife. Satan embraces him and he says: You have done well."

(Muslim, Hadith 2813; authentic)

Repentance: There is Hope

If you are or were involved in this despicable crime, you need to realise one vital thing: All is not lost. Put an end to the affair at once (if you haven't already). Repent. Turn back to Allah. And be prepared to be forgiven by the Almighty.

The Prophet (peace and blessings upon him) said: "Allah, Blessed and Exalted is He, says, 'O son of Adam, as long as you call on Me, I shall forgive you of what you have done, and think nothing of it. O son of Adam, even if your sins were to reach up to the clouds in the sky, and then you were to ask for My forgiveness, I would forgive you and think nothing of it. O son of Adam, even if you were to come to Me with sins nearly as great as the earth, and then you were to meet Me after death, not worshipping anything besides Me, I would bring you forgiveness nearly as great as the earth".

(Tirmidhi, Book 48, Hadith 171; sound)

Subhanallah (Glory be to Allah), how great is our Lord! He loves us so much that He is ever-ready to forgive us no matter the magnitude of our sins, so long as we don't commit *shirk*. All we must do is sincerely feel remorse for the sin that we've committed, discontinue committing it, and repent to Allah with the intention of never returning to the sin again.

Some people have every intention to sin and repent later. This is plain wrong – we cannot be playing games with Allah. Allah informs us of His vast bounty through which He would even convert all of man's sins into good deeds, *provided* the person is sincere in his repentance.

"Except those who repent and believe (in Islamic Monotheism), and do righteous deeds; for those, Allah will change their sins into good deeds, and Allah is Oft-Forgiving, Most Merciful. And whosoever repents and does righteous good deeds; then verily, he repents towards Allah with true repentance"

(Qur'an, 25:70-71)

So hasten to repent to Allah, give up this terrible sin, and perform plenty of righteous deeds.

"Say: 'O 'Ibaadi (My slaves) who have transgressed against themselves (by committing evil deeds and sins)! Despair not of the Mercy of Allah, verily, Allah forgives all sins. Truly, He is Oft-Forgiving, Most Merciful"

(Qur'an, 39:53)

Chapter 3

THE DEVIL'S TRAPS

"Satan said: "Because you have put me in error, I will sit waiting for them on your straight path. Then I will come in from before them and behind them, from their right and from their left, and You will not find most of them grateful".

(Qur'an, 7:16 – 17)

Private Interaction with the Opposite Gender

Speaking to the opposite gender in private (*khalwah*) is certain to bring about a series of problems. This is because the Prophet (peace and blessings be upon him) has warned us of the nature of such a setting:

"A man is not alone with a woman but the third of them is Shaytaan."

(Tirmidhi, Book 33, Hadith 8; authentic)

It is not permissible for a man to correspond with a woman who is not his *mahram* (unmarriageable kin), because of the *fitnah* (temptation) involved in that. It may seem harmless; laughing, joking, and having innocent conversations. But such interactions lead a person from one sin to another. Inappropriate conversations develop and unimaginable events unfold, leaving people many-a-times shocked at their own actions – having done things that they haven't ever conceived themselves of doing.

A person may think that there is no *fitnah* in conversing with a stranger from the opposite sex, but Shaytaan will keep trying until he tempts him into committing much bigger sins.

Social Media

Just as a strange man and woman cannot be in seclusion physically, they are not allowed to be so virtually either. The rules of *khalwah* (seclusion) apply to the internet world too.

Exchanging personal pictures and even indecent images with strangers from the opposite sex over the internet is, sadly, a common phenomenon these days. But this also explains the rising frequency of blackmails and scandals that occur in the cyber world.

No matter how religious, well-intentioned and practising a person may appear on their social media, we never really know the true nature of a person's heart. We have no idea of the disastrous consequences these private conversations can have, but what we do know for sure is that it's not allowed by our Lord. He knows that such interaction will only bring us harm, and has thus forbidden us from entering into them.

So don't feel as though you have to respond to a 'Hi' or 'Hello' from a stranger. You don't. Don't accept friend requests or reply to messages from strange guys or girls. Block them. Make sure that you don't have *non-mahram* guys/girls – including cousins – on your social accounts.

Desist from interacting privately with them and protect yourself and your modesty.

Peer Pressure

Friends can either be a blessing or a test. Your friends may find you strange or weird for not interacting with the opposite gender, for blocking or unfriending them from your social media, and for keeping interactions with *non-mahrams* strictly on a need-to-basis. They may even be surprised when you don't look at every cute-looking girl or guy that walks by to make a comment. You may be mocked for it. Your friends may belittle you, try to convince you to stop being so 'extreme', and may even be the ones that try and set you up with someone. Such friends encourage you to be in relationships that are *haraam* because 'he or she is perfect for you', while they would discourage you from settling down the *halaal* way because 'you are young, free, and should enjoy life'.

When you wish to get closer to Allah, then you have to evaluate your friends circle. If your friends respect you and accept you for your principles, then that is great; but if they constantly try to tempt you and surround you in sin, then the best decision you can make is to seek new friends, those that are fearful of Allah and want to obey Him out of their love for Him. Anyone that cheers you on for doing wrong and entices you into *haraam* relationships is not truly your friend.

"Close friends, that Day, will be enemies to each other, except for the righteous".

23

Find friends that are on the same path as you, those who discourage you from fulfilling false desires, and steer you away from temptation and sin. Don't succumb if your apparently-practising friends are involved in *haraam* relationships. Those who seem to be religious or practising are not our ultimate role models; our guide is the Qur'an and the teachings of the Prophet (peace be upon him). So don't let Shaytaan trick you into validating *haraam* relationships just because your seemingly God-conscious friends are into it. Wanting to 'fit in' can drive a person into *haraam* relationships when they feel as though they are the only ones guarding their chastity whilst everyone around them appears to be happy in their *haraam* relationship. This is only a deception of the Shaytaan. Be mindful of single moments of deception that can plunge you into a lifetime of regret and misery.

Instead, redirect your focus towards developing yourself and your relationship with Allah. Invest your time on self-development, education, work, charity, family and in doing good deeds as much as you can whilst single. Set goals for yourself by enlisting all the things you would like to achieve, and fill your time in doing those tasks so that you don't end up being consumed as someone's girlfriend or boyfriend, and instead find success in fulfilling your life's aspirations. Pursue your dreams, because you never know what you can achieve until you try.

God-conscious friends may be hard to come by these days, but we always have our ultimate friend Allah, our Master. So, dear reader, remain strong and never feel alone.

Insecurity

Don't place your self-esteem in the hands of others. Giving anyone too much power over your own self-regard is mighty dangerous. Because then it is only as long as they flatter you, will you feel good about yourself; once you stop receiving those compliments, your perception of yourself will be ruined. Believe that you are beautiful or handsome, not because of the words of some boy or girl, but because you have been fashioned by none other than Allah.

"We have created man in the best form"

(Qur'an, 95:4)

Do not rely on a boy or a girl to make you feel good about yourself; feel good about yourself because you are you. Learn to love and value your own self. Remember that you don't need to prove yourself to anyone, and if someone makes you feel that you do then you are better off without them. At times, our parents and families may fail to show us just how much they truly love us, even though they do. So if you are seeking love, seek it from Allah, the One that loves you way more than a mother could ever love her child; the One who created you so you could worship Him, the one that you are going to return to. The more you learn about Allah, the more you will fall in love with Him. It is this love that will be your strength and provide you security.

Excuses

One of the most effective traps that Shaytaan lays down is through whispering excuses in the hearts of man. He plants the seeds of doubt and lets it thrive until the heart doesn't find anything wrong with wrong itself. Of course, we do acknowledge that there will inevitably be interactions with the opposite sex, in schools, the university, workplace, etc. However, there shouldn't be *unnecessary* interactions that provide Shaytaan the opportunity to convince one to do more, and eventually exceed the limits set in our religion.

Below are just some of the many excuses man is fooled by Shaytaan into fostering when it comes to mingling with the opposite sex.

'What's the Harm in Looking?'

Growing up, I would hear fellow teenagers say all the time, 'What's the harm in looking?' These young girls and boys were not looking to be in a relationship themselves, but just found no harm in looking; hence, their rhetorical question. Girls and boys were even thought of as 'a bit strange' when they wouldn't ogle all the 'cuties' who were like magnets to everyone else's gaze.

Now older and knowledgeable enough to speak up here is the answer to those teens' question: *There is all the harm in looking.* Making eye contact in general, is one of the most important means of non-verbal communication. It calls attention to a person, and can act as a strong force between two people.

It is noteworthy to observe how Allah connects the issue of lowering the gaze with the issue of protecting the private parts (guarding one's chastity) in the following verses, and how lowering the gaze is mentioned first before protecting the private parts, because the eye influences the heart.

"Tell the believing men to lower their gaze (from looking at forbidden things), and protect their private parts (from illegal sexual acts). That is purer for them. Verily, Allah is All-Aware of what they do. And tell the believing women to lower their gaze (from looking at forbidden things), and protect their private parts (from illegal sexual acts)"

(Qur'an, 24:30-31)

This is why the phrase 'love at first sight' was coined in the first place. It's almost like a spell being cast in the eyes, for one to give their heart away. Letting the gaze wander unhindered can excite the body and make it feel emotions that it shouldn't. The heart begins to crave someone that they may not be able to marry. It makes them vulnerable to fall into sin easily, and it can affect one's whole judgement and lead them to do things they wouldn't normally do.

Gazing at things we shouldn't leads to developing a sickness in the heart that could in turn, lead to immoral actions. It might give you a warm feeling inside when you look at them and you find them returning your gaze. Flirting with the eyes and smiles may seem innocent and fun, but soon it will make you crave for more than just those smiles and looks. Gawking at the opposite sex is destructive to your morals and values, and exceeds the laws of Allah.

Trying to hold on to the concept of 'lowering the gaze' may be particularly challenging in this day and age, with everyone's faces staring right at ours on Facebook, Instagram, and other such platforms. If you are struggling to lower your gaze, consider this piece of advice: either block the person you can't seem to keep your eyes off of, or deactivate your account until you find yourself having more self-control. Like the Prophet (peace be upon him) said, if something disturbs the peace of your heart, then give it up.

Hasan ibn 'Ali (may Allah be pleased with him) said: I memorised from the Messenger of Allah (blessings and peace of Allah be upon him): "Leave that which makes you doubt for that which does not make you doubt, for truth leads to reassurance and lies lead to uncertainty."

(Tirmidhi, Hadith 2442; graded 'authentic' by Al-Albani)

Another sure-fire way of protecting yourself is by unfriending any *non-mahram* from your social media. So many boys have pictures standing with their friends that are girls, commenting on their pictures with heart emojis. This may be a common sight on the net, but is also undeniably unacceptable. Men and women both need to protect their modesty and have *haya* (shame). Hit the block button to every *non-mahram* that is on your following or friends list. Understand that you don't owe anyone any explanations, but

28

you do owe everything to Allah and to yourself. If you feel that a block may come out seeming too harsh with certain people – say, your cousins or friends of the family – then send a polite yet firm message that explains your stance and principles. But beyond that, you don't need to expand on your message and go back and forth in replies. Whatever the case, evaluate the situation and discern the best step to take.

By lowering our gaze from the opposite sex, we protect our eyes from sending unwanted feelings to the heart; by lowering the gaze our chastity is protected, and it will save us from multiple sins. Therefore, it is of utmost importance to lower the gaze and seek refuge in Allah from evil thoughts.

"Allah knows the fraud of the eyes, and all that the breasts conceal"

(Qur'an, 40:19)

'We Are Just Friends'

This is yet another delusion that our youth today are afflicted with.

It might seem alright to hang out and be friends with the opposite sex – especially for a girl that has made it clear to the person that he is in the 'friend zone' and has no chance of getting in any other 'zone'. But the truth is that this is never a fool-proof way of avoiding the dangers of *khalwah* (seclusion). Sadly, many girls learn this the hard way. The more a girl believes that he is just her friend or like a brother to her, the more comfortable she will get with him; texting

29

and chatting with, confiding in, and spending lots of one-on-one time with him because she thinks, 'no one understands me better than him'.

Even though we cannot definitively say that this a ruse that each and every boy plays to get together with a girl, we do learn a lot from the various social experiments conducted in this field.

One such experiment conducted by a couple of non-Muslim students in their university campus springs to mind. In the video experiment, random girls were asked if they could be just friends with a guy, and every girl that was approached answered with a 'yes'. Then a series of boys were asked the same question, but this time – to the surprise of all the girls – the answer was a unanimous 'no'. (*See YouTube video entitled 'Why Men and Women Can't be Friends' by independent filmmakers Jesse Budd and Patrick Romero*).

This is just one of the many experiments done revealing similar results out there. Do your research, and make an objective conclusion for yourself. In saying this, I don't imply that every guy that wants to befriend you does so because he has an ulterior motive, but what I am propounding is that what seems like a harmless friendship can very well develop into a strong attachment and crack open the door leading to a romantic relationship.

Dear sisters, beware of the way a guy's mind works. You don't have to be suspicious of every gesture a guy makes, but don't be naïve of his mentality and possible attempts either.

Be stern and don't pursue conversations any further than they need to go.

'I Know it's *Haraam* but I'm in Love'

Love is an emotion of the heart. It is something that Allah Al-Wadud (The Affectionate) favours His slaves – Muslims and otherwise – with. But it can also be a feeling implanted by the enemy himself, Shaytaan, for the Prophet (peace be upon him) has said: "Satan runs in the body of Adam's son (i.e. man) as his blood circulates in it, and I was afraid that he (Satan) might insert an evil thought in your hearts."

(Bukhari, Book 78, Hadith 243; authentic)

He has also warned us of the dangers of a sick heart, one that is tainted by the whisper of Shaytaan:

"Beware! There is a piece of flesh in the body; if it becomes good (reformed) the whole body becomes good, but if it gets spoilt the whole body gets spoilt – and that is the heart."

(Bukhari, Book 2, Hadith 45; authentic)

So what then determines if this emotion is blessed or wretched? To answer this question, we need to know what love is as defined by Islam.

A Muslim's faith is not complete until the Prophet (peace and blessings of Allah be upon him) is the most beloved person to him in this world.

It was narrated that Anas said: The Prophet (peace and blessings of Allah be upon him) said: "No one of you truly believes until I am dearer to him than his father, his son, his own self and all the people."

(Bukhari, Hadith 15; authentic; Muslim, Hadith 44; authentic)

It was also narrated that 'Abd-Allah ibn Hishaam said: We were with the Prophet (peace and blessings of Allah be upon him) when he was holding the hand of 'Umar ibn al-Khattaab. 'Umar said to him: "O Messenger of Allah, you are dearer to me than everything except my own self."

The Prophet (peace and blessings of Allah be upon him) said: "No, by the One in Whose hand is my soul, not until I am dearer to you than your own self." 'Umar said to him: "Now, by Allah, you are dearer to me than my own self."

The Prophet (peace and blessings of Allah be upon him) said: "Now (you are a true believer), O 'Umar."

(Bukhari, Book 83, Hadith 12; authentic)

As Muslims, we must love Allah and the Prophet (peace and blessings be upon him) first and foremost. And we'd find that our love for all else will follow suit. When we have our priorities straight, our love for other things and people will be in accordance with the teachings of Allah and His Messenger. This is the love that will take us from darkness to light.

Dear brothers and sisters, when you know that it is forbidden to act upon a love that is not allowed yet cannot seem to evade it, ask yourself this question: 'Is my love for Allah lesser than my love for a person that was created by

Him, a person whose heart He controls, and one whose very life belongs to Him?' Because knowing and understanding the severity of this sin and what it leads to yet not giving it up for the sake of Allah is a serious matter indeed.

It is possible to attain the person that you are involved with in a *halaal* (permissible) manner, but by taking the forbidden route, you need to know that the blessings of the relationship would inevitably suffer. When we truly love someone, we wouldn't cause them harm. Therefore if you really love him or her, then why continue the relationship at all knowing very well that every minute you both spend together in privacy would be causing them (and yourself) pain; pain whose effects will be felt both in this life and in the next. Beware of sacrificing your *eeman* (faith) – your greatest blessing, for things that will lead you to Hell.

'I will mislead them and I will create in them false desires...'

(Qur'an, 4:119)

'Our Intention is to Get Married'

All too often people make the mistake of conversing with the person they are considering for marriage for far too long. For years and years marriage was a straightforward affair. It was easier back when families knew each other or *of* each other, and after a few meetings the couple are married. These days when people don't necessarily know the prospect's background in detail, it is very important to get to know them well before marriage, especially since divorce rates are rapidly on the rise. However, such encounters must be done in an Islamic manner with someone responsible being present. Otherwise it can become just like dating.

"When two people (illegally) are together alone then the third is Shaytaan."

(Tirmidhi, Book 33, Hadith 8; authentic)

What needs to be kept in mind is that this person might be a potential spouse, but still *isn't* your spouse. Modesty and *haya* should be practised by both prospects, and they should not be left alone together. We must also keep in mind that no matter how long we speak to someone it isn't going to be possible for a man or a woman to find out about the real character of the other through chatting or spending some time alone together before marriage. It is only natural for people in such situations to show their best side and be on their best behaviour.

It isn't uncommon for those who get married after being engaged in *haraam* relationships to fall into divorce just after a few months or even less than a year or two after marriage. And if the families and parents disapproved of the marriage right from the beginning, then it becomes really easy to just walk away. Shaytaan diabolically pushes the couple together when they are unlawful for one another and pulls them apart when they become lawful for one another. How long will you let him pull your strings? Cut them off now and say 'no' to *haraam* relationships!

Love takes time. It takes time to grow. So beware of making life-time decisions based on infatuation. Ask yourself what you love about them? Are you compatible with each other? Do they possess the qualities you want in the father or mother of your children? Do you trust this person to raise your children well? Think beyond the attraction-factor before you make a decision.

Do not commit the mistake of expecting miracles after marriage. It is very difficult to change someone. If you are not happy with what they are like now, it's highly likely that you won't be so even after ten years of marriage. Imagine yourself married to the person they are now and not what you hope them to be in the future before you decide to tie the knot with them.

When things don't work out, people tend to stay together in the false hope that they will get married to the person eventually. But what they don't realise is that even engaged couples aren't permitted to spend one-on-one time together or interact freely with each other, because until the *nikkah* (marriage) is done both are *non-mahrams* to each other.

Marriage isn't an institution that can be simply leapt into. It needs careful deliberation. So prepare well; educate yourself on the rulings of marriage (and divorce), understand the rights and responsibilities of your spouse, and think as objectively as possible.

'I Want to Help Them in Their *Deen*'

This is a rampant excuse prodded by the Shaytaan. And sadly, this is the excuse that even moderately practising Muslims get affected by. They may view, quite genuinely, interactions with the opposite gender as opportunities to teach them about Islam, to give *da'wah*.

If you feel the same way, then know that although being the one to 'change' someone else can make you feel good about yourself as a striving Muslim, realise that you cannot expect any sort of blessing by using *haraam* means. And here's yet another catch: the more you talk to him or her, the more harm you cause to their faith as well as yours. Such interactions only make things worse. May Allah protect us all.

If you really want them to get closer to Allah and His beautiful *deen* then the best thing you can do is refer them to a trustworthy Muslim of the same sex to speak to and clarify all their doubts with. If you are truly concerned about them, then you'd remove yourself from the equation and make sincere *du'a* for them in their absence.

'He Will Love me if I Sleep With Him'

"Men use love to get sex and woman use sex to get love"

Unknown

A woman may think that if she sleeps with a man, it will cause him to love her and a man believes that when he shows a woman that he loves her she is more likely to sleep with him. Sisters, you have to understand that no matter how much you love him or you think he loves you, it doesn't make it okay to sleep with him. You shouldn't be in a *haraam* relationship in the first place. But if you are and you think that sleeping with him will make him love you and as a result marry you, then you are deceiving yourself.

There are women who, for some strange reason, think it is okay to sleep with a guy if he loves her. But the fact of the matter is that it is never okay to sleep with a guy that isn't your husband. If you are afraid that the man will lose interest in you unless you sleep with him, realise that that is actually a far cry from the truth. He will lose respect for you, and won't value you because you stopped valuing and respecting yourself. This will only increase his appetite to taste other 'fish out there in the sea' because he is done with you now.

Don't even for a moment be fooled into believing that if you give a guy what he wants, he will stop seeking other women's attention. Men can do anything to attain a woman, but they could just as easily drop her soon after they've gotten what they wanted. You owe yourself much more than staying in a state of confusion; you are too precious for that. What you deserve is a husband, not a boyfriend.

Secret Marriages

Secret marriages are basically those marriages conducted in secrecy. Such marriages aren't announced explicitly, instead are hidden from parents, families and the wider community. The two people that witness the marriage are asked to keep silent so that no one finds out about the marriage. All of this goes completely against the practice of marriage in Islam.

Dr. Shaykh Muhammad Akram Nadwi, in an article on Muslim Matters cites the *hadith* of the Prophet (peace and blessings of Allah be upon him): 'Proclaim the marriage'

(*Sunan al-Nasa'i, 3369; Musnad Ahmad, 15697; Sunan Sa`id ibn Mansur, 635*).

Here is a quote of the Shaykh from the same article:

"This a clear injunction that marriages must be proclaimed, made public, not held in secret. That is the practice of the Prophet himself, of all his Companions, and of the prominent scholars of the early generations. None of them ever indulged in secret marriages and they never, explicitly or tacitly, approved any such marriages…This is the opinion of al-Zuhri: 'If someone marries secretly, brings two witnesses but commands them to keep it secret, it would be obligatory to separate the husband and wife'. Similarly, it is reported that Imam Malik's opinion is that non-proclamation of marriage invalidates the marriage (*al-Mughni, k. al-nikah*)."

The person proposing the idea of a secret marriage may either be simply ignorant, assuming that it is something acceptable in Islam, or they may be nothing short of deceitful, seeking to fulfil their ulterior motives. Secret marriages are not a temporary cure or fix; they are a hidden disease and the cause of long-term regrets. Being approached with a prospect that asks you to keep the marriage a secret should immediately set off alarm bells in your mind. Be warned that you are entering a danger zone if you do plan to go ahead with it. How do you know that there aren't other women the person is also in secret marriage(s) with? Moreover, when nobody knows about your marriage, then you can't expect to receive the rights or security that belongs to a wife. At the end of the day, both men and women should take responsibility not to be convinced of a secret marriage. Please don't allow your emotions to lead you into a path that has no light at the end of the tunnel.

I would like to shed light in this section on the concept of secret marriages as proposed by well-known speakers. Sisters, I advise you to be all the more careful if a renowned or "trusted" Muslim preacher proposes to you for entering into a secret marriage. Do not be blinded by his knowledge or apparent sincerity. Islam's stance on secret marriages is enough to deter us from entering into such marriages – no matter how convincingly the preacher seems to put forward his proposal. Unfortunately, such men can easily use their fame to take advantage of a student. I don't mean to say that every single preacher has malicious motives, rather, the ones who give in to Shaytaan's whispers can very well use the trust and faith they have developed in the eyes of their followers over the years for their own benefit. It is a sad reality that this is becoming a trend in the Muslim *ummah* – where preachers and speakers misuse the respect they have earned for lowly gains. It is these types of 'scholars' that I refer to in this section.

Some people in the field of *da'wah* (calling to Islam) are notorious for taking up secret marriages on their travels around the world as if they were sipping on cups of tea. They possibly think of themselves as clever for utilising an alternative – perhaps they consider it a 'loop hole' in Islam, *na'udhu billah* (we seek refuge in Allah) – for committing *zina*, and that they have figured a way to take out their desires on vulnerable women who have no permission from their *wali* (legal guardian), while the witnesses of the secret marriage are sworn to secrecy. And once they're done with their secret spouse, they discard them nonchalantly over a text message.

When it comes to celebrated Muslim speakers, many of us have a blind spot. We want to believe the promises that these people make when they come forward with their illegitimate proposals, even though our instincts may go against it. We rush to give them the benefit of the doubt, because we've fallen in love with their talks, and in turn with the prospect of spending our life with them – so much that we end up sacrificing our dignity, our rights as women and as human beings. My dear sisters, this is why we have to stay alert and be on our guard.

40

It's truly heart-breaking to see some of the preachers that we respect so much not practice what they themselves preach, and it's devastating to realise that they don't for a minute consider the emotional trauma caused by this so-called marriage, which only shatters a woman's dreams of a happy marriage.

But after all that is said and done, what we need to do is train ourselves to react appropriately for when this tragic reality does occur. We must not end up questioning our faith because of the actions of a few speakers. No matter how good their speech is, only Allah knows the condition of someone's heart. People with evil intent – no matter what walk of life they come from – will find any way possible to carry out their evil. This is why it is crucial that we don't attach our faith to a preacher but to Allah alone.

The fact that many people out there are corrupt shouldn't make us corrupt when dealing with them. Instead we hold on to the Rope of Allah tighter than ever before, and return to His Book and its divine injunctions. We strive to develop a special bond with our Creator through the Qur'an, *du'a*, and *adkaar*, and by emulating the role models that Islam has provided us for eternity, instead of placing the fate of our faith in the hands of a preacher that can go rogue at any time. We don't need someone from this particular era to be the *epitome* of role models for us, since we already have in our *deen* timeless role models for men, women and all of humanity who will not betray our trust or let us down – the Prophets (peace be upon them), our Mothers – the wives of the Prophet (peace be upon him and them) and also the *Sahaba* (may Allah be pleased with them).

<hr/>

Allah's Laws are placed to protect us from unforeseen harm; they are not there to make our lives hard. On the contrary, they are there to make our lives easier. When you start to truly believe this, you will have a positive mind-set and will readily avoid the forbidden.

"Allah intends for you ease and does not intend for you hardship"

(Qur'an, 2:185)

What we must remember is that we all have a choice, and the choices that we make have the power to either light up the sky of our world or scar our lives and those of our families for a very long time. Do not allow sweet words of others, or your own desires, emotions, and blind faith in a person destroy your life. When it comes to marriage, remember to involve your *wali*, make the families meet, and announce the wedding ceremony. Be warned of marriages that have no *wali*, as such are marriages devoid of blessings and peace. What is important to note is that when it comes to marriage, the decision should be made with a clear mind, not one that is blinded by love and deafened with sweet words.

Dear brother, if you really want to become a 'man', get married. Dear sister, if you really want a man who will love you and commit to you, get married. Don't sell your chastity, dignity and modesty for what you perceive to be love but isn't. Have *sabr* (patience); it will most definitely be worth it *In Sha Allah*.

May Allah grant us and our offspring the best of marriages and protect us from everything that causes harm. Aameen.

Chapter 4

THE PLAYERS

By now you would, *In Sha Allah*, be convinced that *haraam* relationships are completely forbidden, and that there is no reason to get into one as all the good intentions we may have and the excuses we give ourselves in this pursuit are actually baseless. The end result is the same; it's wrong and it will never be right.

In many relationships, people are played by others who have a 'game plan'. For such players, it isn't about love more than it is about conquests. They want a game to play and they choose vulnerable preys as pawns in their game. These types of people don't have a moral compass; it doesn't matter whether you are a good Muslim, from a decent family, or even that you are a fellow human being. It's just about one thing to them and that is their ego. Winning others over is a challenge for them – all part of their fun and games. They will chase a person until they can make them give in. This is why it is highly important to be aware of these types of people and the game that they play in order to safeguard ourselves.

Luckily, we all have our gut feeling that pops in to rescue us from dangerous situations. It is up to us to acknowledge this little voice signalling that something is not quite right. Don't be quick to dismiss it. Rather, listen closely to it and listen carefully. It is there for a reason.

This chapter is dedicated to helping you hone that voice, tune into it and ultimately save yourself from the rollercoaster of hell by guarding your heart and protecting yourself from *haraam* relationships; and if you are in one already, then by breaking away from it.

The Game

Recognising the various methods that certain people use in their 'game plan' is one of the powerful ways to freeing one from false attachments. It is one of the guaranteed paths that lead to the freedom and protection of one's heart and *eeman*. In the following section, I will enlist some of the many manipulative techniques employed by players in their game.

The Biggest Lie

The biggest lie used by emotional predators for the longest time in history has probably been the infamous words: I LOVE YOU. And secondly: I WILL MARRY YOU.

Many people fall in love with an illusion, confusing lust and infatuation for love. Studies reveal that when the brain is in a state of lust, it is much like a brain on drugs. MRI scans illustrate that the same area lights up when an addict gets a fix of cocaine as when a person is experiencing the intense lust of physical attraction. When you experience lust, you don't see the person for who they really are, rather you see the person in the light you would *want* them to be.

Most girls believe that they truly are in love when they utter these words but lamentably, for most boys these words are merely bait that they use to catch the ones they want to romance with, take theirs desires out on and simply have some fun with.

Guys use these words almost like a spell to cast upon their victims. They might be your cousin, your relative, your neighbour, even your best friend – but at the end of the day they are just boys who aren't man enough to marry you; so instead of offering marriage they offer you a *haraam* relationship and *zina*.

Girls can be really naïve when they fail to understand an average guy's mentality. They believe that the boy must indeed love her back when he showers her with attention. Sure, he may love the way you look, the way you dress, the way your hair smells, and even the way you look on his arm, but it is far from love in the sense that you understand it to be. Infatuation is superficial love, something that is based on outward appearance rather than the inward.

Whereas if a guy knows that you are not into the dating scene, he may try to get to you from the 'I will marry you' angle. He may convince you that he wants to marry you although he has very little intention of doing so; he won't come to your house to bring forward his proposal yet he would want to 'get to know you better' by spending time

46

with you, and then when he's had enough, he'd move on to someone else.

Dear sisters, be wise. Do not fall for this trick. If you are looking for true love, know that you will find it only through the love of Allah – the love for Him and the love for His sake. If you have Allah's love with you, then you will have a healthy dose of love for yourself in the present, and will make way for a blessed love with your husband in the future as well. So don't let the love that will only deceive and hurt you get in your way right now.

Mind Games

Mind games come in many forms but what they all have in common is the signals used to toy with a person's emotions. Players love messing with other's feelings. They recognise how emotions can affect people and take advantage of it. They play mind games because it is 'fun' for them and they find it amusing to keep the other confused and unstable. Players find satisfaction in throwing others off balance.

Most of us have grown up watching Disney and Hollywood movies that have had an impact on us and our perception of love. Girls, especially, begin to believe that they need a man to make them feel complete and that there is something missing when there isn't one in their lives. It keeps them longing for someone special and from even a very young age, most girls dream about getting married and being whisked away by that someone special. This leads to blind trust and hope in the first man that professes love for them.

47

Players try to get your attention by being 'different', so you find them interesting. Some may play hard-to-get and instead of showering you with compliments, may withhold any such compliments because they want you to view them differently from other men.

And if you get dumped, be careful. Being dumped could lead to "frustration attraction" which means that the person who was dumped will love and lust the person who dumped them even more than before. I recommend you to do your research and find out more about this.

Marriage is a great *sunnah* (Prophetic practice), and *alhamdulliah* there are great men out there, so please do not lose hope. If you do things the wrong way then you will find the wrong men in your life, but if you do things the right way then *In Sha Allah* you will find the right man come into your life through *halaal* means; a man who is serious about commitment and worthy of you.

Catfishing

Catfishing is a type of deceptive activity involving a person creating a puppet social networking presence for nefarious purposes. Catfishing can be part of a romance scam. It is a way for some online users to trick people into believing that they are someone that they are not. The catfish uses someone else's identity i.e. photos that they have taken from other social media accounts to form a relationship with their target or to pursue numerous relationships online.

The victim of catfishing may think they have a genuine relationship with the person on the other side of the screen, but they are oblivious to the fact that the person in most cases is using a fake profile, fake photos, a fake name and usually a fake story which they have conspired to trick the person into having a romantic relationship or friendship with them. In some cases, the person may even pretend to be from among the opposite gender. It's a very messy situation.

The trap works when the victim is gullible and/or when the catfish is such a good liar that there seems no reason to doubt that they are who they say they are.

This just reinforces the reason as to why we shouldn't form online relationships with strangers. We would only be fooling ourselves when we believe that it isn't sinful or that there is nothing wrong with it because there is distance and no physical relationship. However, in Islam all intimate relationships – real or virtual – are prohibited before marriage.

Blackmailing

Blackmail is generally considered to be socially unacceptable, yet it happens in different ways in many relationships. It is easy for those who have some form of control to use the power this tactic gives in a threatening way. Blackmail can also be subtle, with hints of negative consequences rather than direct threats.

Emotional blackmail is a form of psychological manipulation that employs a mixture of threats, appeals and emotionally punitive controlling behaviour. Under pressure from emotional blackmail, one may become a sort of hostage, forced to act against their will.

Emotional blackmailers play with the feelings, fears and weaknesses of their victims. They exploit common fears in people to get them to do what they want. They may appear to be charming as they put on their best impersonation of a friendly person around others. The deception lies is in how they make you out to be the one with the problem.

When we don't comply to do what the blackmailer wants us to, they may feel that it is necessary to use threats and apply pressure until we cave in. However, if we agree to their demands, then we are giving them power over us and no doubt they will do the same thing repeatedly, in order to have complete dominance over us.

If we acknowledge that the only reason blackmail can occur is because we are allowing it to happen and we have made the choice to give that power over us to someone else then we can reform our choice and take that power back, either by walking away from that person or increasing our resistance to manipulation. We must also be willing to accept the consequences of this and keep firm. No matter how bad the weapon they try to use against us is, no matter how much worse their threats become, we must be willing to face it, keep firm, and not give in. This will eliminate the power they have and will make it clear to them that they can't control us.

Talk to a friend whom you are certain you can trust. Talk to an approachable family member or teacher. If you need to get an older person or someone with authority from the community to help you, don't be shy to call out. And don't hesitate to call a confidential helpline or even the police if you have to.

Think about what you're going to do. Take your confidants' suggestions into account. Make a plan, and assure yourself that the plan can't go wrong and it won't be anything that you will regret, *In Sha Allah* (Allah willing).

Remember: if you give into them then you have given them the power of endless emotional abuse. It is our attachment to things which enables others to blackmail us with them. If we didn't have this attachment, it wouldn't be possible to blackmail us. So emotionally detach yourself from whatever it is they are blackmailing you with, and free yourself from their snare.

Types of Players

Some players try to be the soul of the party, always complimenting, smiling and telling jokes to everyone aiming to impress their target by presenting a false image of themselves, while other players would tease a girl by pointing out her flaws to 'knock her off her high horse', bringing her down to his level without a guard so that she can be easily be manipulated. This shows the different levels that players can resort to in order to get a girl any way they can.

Under this section, we will explore a few such types of players out there.

The 'Friend'

Many players (often the menfolk) get into the 'game' through friendship. They are patient enough to stay in the 'friend zone' whilst they plan every move to play their prey. They become their closest friend. Such men talk about their problems, past relationships and heartbreaks trying to get the girl feel sorry for them. They will make her believe that since they have been hurt, they would never hurt; since they have been betrayed, they would never betray. The player may even go as far as making her believe that he is actually in love with someone else just to avoid any suspicions from arising in her mind. The culprit uses this time to plan his next move. Then, if things go as they usually do in these cases, the victim finds herself gradually falling in love with her player until they both end up together.

While things may seem to go well at the start of the relationship, it would eventually lead to the many inevitable pits that are present in *haraam* relationships. The player floods his victim with love and attention, and she feels that she has found 'the one' and begins to trust him (a tad too much). At this stage, he knows that he's hooked her in and that's when he suddenly leaves her hanging. There is no talk of marriage, and no time for the girl anymore. He constantly wants a break, and can meet her only when he wants to. This makes her feel lonelier than she felt even before the relationship, and she begins to lose herself a little every day. She doesn't recognise who she is anymore, and her family and friends don't either. She loses her smile, her spark and everything that made her 'her' to him. This is the damage that a 'friend' can cause.

Married Players

Yet another type of player is the married one. It's astonishing how many people are involved with married people!

The victim might not even know that the player is married. By the time they do finally find out, they may be too emotionally involved in the relationship. At that point, they would want to do anything to stay with them and believe whatever excuse they come up with to justify their infidelity to their wife. They would rather believe the player's callous lies because they are now too emotionally attached to throw the relationship to the curb.

The player could be happily married but they'd pretend to be otherwise. They would also provide a ton of excuses to keep the forbidden relationship going while the victim is ready to believe them all just so it eases the guilt.

Some of the many excuses that male married players use are:

- ✖ "I wish I met you first. Then I wouldn't have married her"

- ✖ "She is a monster, who doesn't deserve me"

- ✖ "I'm not physical with her"

- ✖ "She has an illness. I can't leave her just yet"

- ✖ "She will suicide if I leave her"

- ✖ "I haven't divorced her because of the children"

- ✗ "I'm in the process of a divorce" or "I will divorce her soon"

The majority of married men never leave their wives. In fact, the statistics on infidelity conducted by the Associated Press under the *Journal of Marital and Family Therapy* in 2016 cites that 57% of men admitted to committing infidelity in any relationship they've had. The longer someone remains in such a *haraam* relationship – the punishment of which is severer than just two unmarried – the longer they will suffer.

Online Players

In today's technologically advanced world, online players are by far the most rampant. Social media sites are like candy stores for online players. They have so many different girls to choose from to make their prey. Getting girls to fall in love with, and fawn over them is their mission. The more hearts they break, the bigger their ego. So they approach their victims as 'wolves in sheep's clothing'. They first find out who the victim is and the type of person that they are looking for. Then they resort to charming the victim using endless flattery.

Here is a true story in this regard of a young man from the UK who spent tons of effort and time in making a young lady from Pakistan his girlfriend. After relentlessly pursuing her and finally getting her to fall in love with him over the internet, he arranged to meet her. Once they met, he slept with her and never contacted her ever again.

Allah alone knows how many more such awful stories there are. No doubt, horrific events such as this happen all the time, which is why women, especially, should be careful not to get fooled into falling for someone's fake love and attraction.

We all have days in our lives when we feel lonely. And at those times, when we happen to receive messages from people constantly contacting us and wooing us on our social media, it is only natural to feel loved. After all, who doesn't love a compliment, especially when they need it most? But know this my dear sister: these expressions of love are not real. They are just traps being laid out for you. The online predator hopes that you eventually give him a chance, befriend him, and exchange numbers. He makes it seem innocent because you are not doing anything physical – not yet, anyway. And you oblige because you wonder why he would invest so much time in you if he wasn't at all serious in the first place.

What we need to understand is that we may think that talking to men online isn't a big deal. On the flip side though, constantly gazing at someone's face (even if it be just their picture), flirting with them, and getting all sorts of 'fuzzy feelings' when they comment/tweet about us, in reality, *is* a big deal. In such cases, the young lady gets emotionally invested and starts to expect 'like's, 'heart's and compliments; and when she doesn't receive them, she begins to doubt her self-worth.

Some women may think that they can change the player if they just hold on long enough, that he'd eventually turn around and choose her to be his 'one and only'. But truth be told, one can never change a player; a player has to do that for himself. And the longer a girl lets a guy play her, the more suffering she'd cause herself, and the more time it'd take to get over him. Remind yourself, dear sister, that if he is serious about you, then he will most definitely contact your *wali* (guardian) regarding marriage, instead of wasting your time talking about a marriage that he never truly planned to be a part of.

I believe that it is vital for single girls to refrain from making themselves so readily available on social media. What I mean by this is to beware of making it easy for people to see your pictures and view your personal information. Keep yourself and the details about yourself private and viewable by girls (whom you know) only.

As for the men, my humble request to you is to unfriend all the *non-mahram* women that you have in your contacts. The above message is just as important for and applies wholly to you as it does to the ladies.

Narcissists

Psychologist Stephen Johnson writes that a narcissist is someone who has "buried his true self-expression in response to early injuries and replaced it with a highly developed, compensatory false self".

A relationship with a narcissist is a dangerous one. It is unlike any other relationship. In such a relationship, the victim is psychologically played with to the extreme. For this reason, we must inform ourselves of the different phases and signs that such a relationship entails in order to steer clear from it.

The Idealisation Phase: This is the very first phase. The narcissist places the victim on a high pedestal, making them the centre of their world. The narcissist will make frequent contact with their victim and shower them with flattery and praise. At this stage, the victim won't for a moment think ill of this person, and may even go over and above in believing that they have met their soul mate.

Things to look out for in this stage are: constant texting, shallow flattery, and wanting to be around you at all times, among others. This is a technique known as 'love-bombing' and it is how most victims get sucked in. In this way, the narcissist fools the victim into thinking that they are interested in them, when in truth, the predator is only interested in making them dependent on his/her constant praise and attention.

The Devaluation Phase: During this stage of the relationship with the narcissist, the victim is left wondering why they are abruptly thrown off the pedestal and abandoned. The narcissist suddenly starts to blow hot and cold. They stonewall their victim, emotionally withdrawing from them and give them the silent treatment when the victim fails to meet their extreme "standards". The narcissist makes them believe that they are the one that is at fault and that they need to make changes in themselves to please the narcissist. They feed off of other people's misery and pain just as they feed off of their admiration.

The narcissist demeans the victim in order to maintain control over them. They mislead their victim into thinking that if they stop being so "needy" or "clingy", then they will love them back the way they did at the beginning of the relationship.

The more one chases after a narcissist, the more the narcissist pulls away. They disappear more frequently and give the victim the silent treatment in an attempt to create distance. They will give their victim crumbs of their attention – just enough to keep them emotionally invested and available to them. The victim feels like the narcissist's punching bag. Constantly criticised, put down, and compared to others, the victim is left mourning the idealisation phase. He/she doesn't realise that the person that they met at the beginning of their relationship doesn't exist; it was all a façade, an act put on in order to 'secure their supply'.

The Discard Phase: By now, the victim is an emotional wreck, constantly asking himself/herself: "Did he/she ever love me? Did I mean anything to him/her?" The answer to which is a flat 'no'. The victim was no more than an object to the narcissist. The narcissist also wants the victim to feel worthless. So he/she may spread rumours about their victim, hurt them intentionally, cheat on them, and insult and disrespect them.

Narcissists will never take responsibility for their actions; they simply don't care how they have treated their victim or how they are feeling. Those that are unfamiliar with the narcissistic disorder are completely at a loss to understand how cruel their behaviour is.

The victim needs to understand that they were deliberately targeted, lied to and manipulated by the narcissist. That is how a narcissist functions. So the best way to deal with one is to go contact-free with them. Should the victim break free, they will try to contact them again at some point (maybe when they are bored). And depending on when they broke free from the narcissist they are only a shadow of their former self, with a lot of work ahead of them to rebuild their broken self-image. So if you, dear reader, are stuck in this rut, be on your guard and don't give in to those incoming texts or calls. In that regard, I would recommend you to change your number, or block them from your mobile phone, social media and all other ways through which they could contact you.

Here are a couple more techniques that a narcissist uses which we must be aware of:

Gas-lighting: This is a technique abusers use to convince their victim that their perception of the abuse is inaccurate. Their intention is to invalidate and criticise the victim's emotions, and place the blame on them. As victims are led to mistrust their own instincts, they end up staying in the abusive relationship, believing that they are the ones at fault.

The Smear Campaign: A narcissist is shrewd. They make their victims believe that they are the unstable ones in the relationship. They even depict them to be the abusive or the crazy partner in front of others and in doing so, intend to prod the victim into frantically defend themselves against this portrayal of them, nipping the chance to showcase their 'instability' in front of others.

The best thing the victim can do, as mentioned previously, is to go contact-free with the predator and move forward. The victim must see themselves as not only a victim but a survivor of this terrible abuse. This will make the healing process easier and help them rebuild their life.

Personality Disorders

We meet different types of people in life. Among them are the ones that can break you – the destructive people. It is important to understand different personalities as it may give you answers to the questions you've always had as to why you were treated so badly. There are many disturbing personality types out there; enlisting and explaining each one would require a separate book of its own. Hence I request you, dear reader, to do your own research on sociopathic, psychopathic, and other such anti-social personalities. I guarantee you that it would be a highly educative search.

How to Spot a Player

There are certain protective measures that boys and girls need to take, and just cannot do without in today's world.

One such measure would be to educate ourselves of the signs of a player.

As humans we are in fact, fallible and can easily get tempted and fall weak, which is why I warn you of this. Even the girls that never think they will fall into this sin are tricked into it. They struggle heavily despite their faithful upbringing and may end up messing their lives up for someone they wrongly believe to be the 'love of their life'.

Pay attention to these signs of players (including but not limited to the following):

✗ They don't talk about (or try their best to avoid any conversations on) marriage. They are rather interested in when you'd be meeting them next.

✗ They make excuses as to why they can't get married to you and often say, 'Maybe in the future'.

✗ Neither does the man talk to your *wali* (guardian) nor does he have any immediate plan to.

✗ They don't take you seriously and everything is on their terms.

✗ They don't discuss family issues with you.

✗ They ask you for indecent images, want to see you without your *hijab* (Islamic garb), and/or tempt you into doing obscene things with them.

✗ They will present themselves to be everything that you want a good partner to be and may even promise marriage to rope you in.

- ✘ You are a challenge to them. It could be gaining your emotional attachment, acquiring physical intimacy with you, or any other such feats that they consider a challenge to be won.

- ✘ They have you fall in love with them only to finally drop you out of their lives. Once they have gotten what they want from you (or miserably failed out of frustration or boredom), they will disappear. Players will play if they get what they want. If not, they won't waste any time in walking out.

- ✘ They make you feel paranoid or make it seem as you are the problem and that they need some space from the relationship.

- ✘ They like to show you off to their friends, as though you are an object of interest to them. They might even seek the approval of their friends to see if you 'make the cut'.

- ✘ They don't answer your calls, and don't bother to reply to your messages.

- ✘ They don't let you touch their phone or trust you with their social media passwords.

- ✘ They are openly flirtatious with others and come across as real charmers.

Recall that when a person truly loves you they show interest in things that are important to you and disclose things that are important to them. They would want to know about your family, friends, and generally about how your life has been so far and how you want it to be in the future. But for players, it's just about the present because they don't intend to have you in their lives long term.

Every time you want to meet with your man *(which you shouldn't be doing in the first place)*, he refuses claiming to be busy. It would seem as though he is busy with just about everything but you. For all you know, he may be busy in dating and luring other girls as well into his game. He either got what he wanted from you, or maybe he didn't, but that won't stop him from moving on to someone else. The truth is if you think that he is cheating on you, or that he is a player, you are probably right. There is a reason why you doubt him. So go with your inner voice lest you later regret it.

Incredibly, there are multiple books and blogs that outline on how to be a player. Women, especially, must research on this to get an insight into players' minds so that they may be alert and stay several steps ahead of their game.

Dear reader, I wish that you never have to come across a player or his traps. Yet I write this solely because we know that the devil does all he can to tempt the human heart. And since emotions are strong and since love can blind, it could lead you to doing things that you thought you never would. People are quick to assume that this won't happen to them (and *In Sha Allah* it won't) but none of us know what the future holds or what we will be tested with so we must strengthen our guard and prepare for the worst by educating ourselves on this. So before someone tricks you into giving them your heart protect it by learning about the minds of players.

Why Some People are Players

Players are very different from what they portray themselves to be to the outside world. On the inside, players are people that want to attract everyone around them and who, unfortunately, usually succeed.

What players desperately seek is approval. They come across as confident but really have low self-esteem and are on a mission to elevate their self-worth by collecting as many lovers as possible. Players are so insecure about the value of their own self that they need multiple people telling them that they love them, and fawn over them to feel important. They want to feel needed. Such people have unmet needs and doubts about themselves. And the only way for them to get rid of these doubts is to gather as many admirers as they can. In short, they mask their shortcomings by hiding behind the identity of a player so that they can feel worthy.

Another reason for people becoming players is that they have had their hearts broken in the past. They feel that having been wronged makes it their prerogative to wrong others. Their logic is: "My life was 'messed up'. Therefore I am entitled to 'mess up' others' lives." They are hurting deep inside. But what makes them blameworthy is their notion that the only way to get back self-control is by inflicting pain and hurt on others.

This happens a lot amongst both guys and girls. People tend to lose their self-worth when their significant other leaves them. So they try to fill that void by playing with the lives of others. They don't want to deal with emotional connections or commitments anymore so they pretend and do whatever they can to be the one to outsmart this time. In doing so, some guys go after the most practising or 'the good girl' just to break her and fulfil some sickening objective. They get an ego boost as they convince their victim that they are the real deal when in reality they are nothing but a fraud.

We need to pity such souls; how sad is it that someone can't be their true selves, that they have to lie, cheat, manipulate and trick someone to fall in love with them, only to finally betray them. That is not a confident man or woman. That is a very broken person whom we should pity, and not pine over.

For other players, it's about being Mr Popular. They like to show off to their friends the number of girls pining after them, and the demand for their attention. Low-life friends are impressed by such guys and put them on a pedestal. But those who have true self-respect and respect for human life in general will see them for the ruthless and disgusting rogues that they are.

It's safe to say that if you have been played you were not the problem; they were. You are not at fault for being fooled. However, your mistake lies in disobeying Allah, in turning a blind eye to His Laws, and in giving into your desires instead of surrendering to Him. No matter how good one's intentions are disobeying Allah will not bring any success or progression in one's life.

Then again, we are all humans who make mistakes and fall into or are tricked into sin. The solution lies in seeking forgiveness from your Lord and also in forgiving yourself. Don't be harsh on yourself; you need your own love and support the most to bounce back from this trial. And do not wait for the trickster to come back to you – he just may, but not to give you the love that you need, instead to play you all over again. Be kind to yourself and vow to never make the same mistake again.

An Important Message for the Brothers

If you are a brother who has played girls before, are doing so now, or even consider it alright to do so, please take this section as my sincere advice and admonition to you.

A fling is something you may think you want. But in reality, it isn't what you *need* to keep you happy in the long run; it could turn out to be one of the biggest things you will regret in life.

Sadly, the society that we live in today is always harder on the girls than it is on the boys, particularly when it comes to dating. This consequently leaves the girl more vulnerable because *her* sin is – very unfairly – deemed more blameworthy by the culprit himself that initiated this forbidden relationship let alone the uneducated members of the community. It is easier to blame the girl since 'it is because of *her fitnah* that the man refused to lower his gaze and ultimately lured her.

Yet this is precisely why the men should never take this sin lightly, and why they should be concerned twice as much – because while girls are constantly reminded of what to do and what not to do, the men aren't. In fact quite often, and quite shockingly, their shameful behaviour is celebrated and triumphed upon by the society. Know that you cannot get away with casual relationships even if you have your parents' or the society's approval. They may not consider it a crime, but it is most definitely one in the Sight of Allah. Allah is infinitely just. He will see to it that they are recompensed for the sin that they've gone scot-free for all their lives. So beware of a day that will come when you will have to pay a heavy price for taking advantage of girls and using them.

Brothers need to take this issue seriously. Unfortunately, many guys find it alright to abuse a woman and do whatever he wishes with her. But the Laws set by Allah should really put fear into every man (and woman) and make them rethink their interaction with the opposite gender no matter how 'innocent' it may seem.

Dear brother, know that if you have played with girls callously, then you have indeed murdered people's trust, their dreams, and their reputation. You have stabbed them in their hearts and scarred them for almost life. Is this all just because you couldn't restrain yourself? Were you so weak that you had to lie, betray, and ultimately destroy someone's life – just because you couldn't control your desires?

It is cowards that try to impress their friends by the number of girls they have dated. Real men neither brag, nor give into the pressure of their friends. Only someone that's got something to hide will try to prove how 'manly' he is. But remember that being a real man means to protect and respect women. A real man is strong enough to control his desires; a weak man only cares about what his friends think.

If you are the type that dumped the girl once she reciprocated interest, finding her to be too 'loose', remind yourself that it is you who awoke the desire in her in the first place; it is you that lured her into your trap of friendship and then made false promises of marriage. So why do you then think low of her when her heart weakened and got addicted to you? Why do you feel that she is not good enough for you anymore? Is it because girls should be free from sexual thoughts? Is having little to no sexual drive what makes a girl 'pure'?

Have you forgotten your elaborate scheming that led the girl into your trap? Do you wish to dismiss the countless number of times that she's resisted when you tried to seduce her? Yet you persisted with your false promises and fake charm, until all her walls were knocked down. After all that, do you dare accuse her of being the 'impure' one? One cannot touch something pure with dirty hands and then question its purity.

Men are meant to be the protectors of women, not those who disrespect women. If a Muslim woman does something that isn't deemed appropriate, then do not help Shaytaan against her by degrading or cursing her. Brothers, these women are your sisters in Islam, and if non-Muslim, then they are your sisters in humanity. A woman, no matter what faith she is a part of, never deserves to be used or abused.

It was narrated from Abu Hurairah that the Messenger of Allah said:

"Avoid the seven sins that doom one to Hell." It was said: "O Messenger of Allah, what are they?" He said: "Associating others with Allah (Shirk), magic, killing a soul whom Allah has forbidden killing, except in cases dictated by Islamic law, consuming riba, consuming the property of orphans, fleeing on the day of the march (to battlefield), and slandering chaste women who never even think of anything touching their chastity and are good believers."

(Sunan al-Nasa'i, Book 30, Hadith 61; authentic)

When a woman says no, she means no. Please do not harass her, whether she is dressed modestly in your opinion, or not. If you chase her, and she finally gives into the temptation, then what right do you have to blame her for the game you had played? Remember, she is only human like you. You have no right to call her names or deface her honour. And when your friends talk down to a girl or show disrespect towards her please have the courage to correct them; do not facilitate the oppression of women by keeping silent or worse, by joining in.

Respected brother, question and take your own self to account. Wake up from your slumber and fear Allah. In our gender-biased society's eyes, you may get away easily with your sins. But in reality, your sins and those of a woman are no different from each other; her sins are no worse than yours. One can never be certain, maybe your sin is far worse in the Sight of Allah because of your ill intentions right from the beginning, your intentional scheming, and your lack of regret and remorse.

Oh brother, fear Allah, because everyone's evil actions will catch up with them sooner or later; today, tomorrow, in the future – or worse yet, *aakhirah*. So repent sincerely and change your ways. And vow to never string anyone along again.

Your honour lies in the honour of the women of the *ummah;* if you play a part in ripping apart a women's honour, you are ripping apart your own honour. Remember to treat other women the way you would like your own mother, or sister to be treated. Protect them and stick up for them the way you would do for your own. May Allah accept your repentance, help you undo what you did wrong, and guide you to His Straight Path. *Aameen.*

Chapter 5

BREAK AWAY

"As for the one who is conscious of Allah, He prepares for him a way out. And He provides for him from sources that he could never imagine."

(Qur'an, 65:2 – 3)

Many people stay in relationships due to the fear of losing their 'only means of a happy and fulfilled life'. They pin all their hopes and dreams onto one person whom they believe is the only way to their happiness. What they fail to realise is that true happiness does not come from *haraam* things; it does not come from people. Instead, true happiness comes from obeying Allah and His Laws alone.

It might seem like the hardest thing to do, but you can do it. And once you start, you will be amazed at how Allah makes things that initially appeared to be difficult for you, easy.

You CAN break away. And here's how.

Set your *Niyyah*

Set your intention straight. You no longer want to be involved in such a lowly sin – only for the sake of Allah. It doesn't matter whether they treat you right or wrong. Just

71

the fact that they are in touch with you and you with them outside of a marital contract, makes it unequivocally wrong.

Be sincere in your intention to break up so that you can stay steadfast well into the future, and avoid making the same mistake later.

Dear reader, make your love for Allah greater and more precious than your love for a boyfriend or girlfriend, which may very well lead you into the Fire (may Allah preserve you). Your fear of Allah is enough to become your strength for doing the right thing.

Know that if you give up something for the sake of Allah, He will give you something better. Believe in this principle whole-heartedly, and recall the story of Umm Salamah, a companion (may Allah be pleased with her) whose most beloved husband passed away, and she made *du'a* to Allah for receiving something better in return:

"Inna lillahi wa inna ilaihi raji`un. Allahumma ujurni fi musibati, wakhluf li khairan minha"

(We belong to Allah and to Him we shall return. O Allah! Compensate me in my affliction, recompense my loss and give me something better in exchange for it)

(Muslim, Book 7, Hadith 921; authentic)

Few months later, she (may Allah be pleased with her) ended up marrying the best of all creations – Prophet Muhammad (peace and blessings be upon him) himself! *Allahu Akbar (Allah is Great)*.

So keep praying for something better. And Allah will surely reward you with nothing less than the best.

Take Action

End the relationship immediately.

Make it abundantly clear to the person with whom you are in this *haraam* relationship that the only option is marriage for you, and to not contact you anymore, but to contact your parents if they were ever serious about the relationship with you. No ifs ands or buts.

You don't need to give anyone any explanations. Simply saying, "I've repented to Allah and I am ending this relationship now" before cutting of all contact is the best thing to do. And if you know that they are serious about marriage, then saying something along the lines of: "Please contact my *wali* (guardian) for a proposal. I no longer want to be in any sort of *haraam* relationship, so don't contact me personally" is more than enough. It is important that this is the last and final thing you say to them. Do not give them the opportunity to start a conversation with you lest you end up where you started. Block them, or change your number so that they understand that the only way to get to you is by the permission of your *wali* via marriage proposal. Having said that, do not wait around for them to do this. Move on with your life and don't put it on pause for anyone.

The next step would be to block the person from your phone and social media. And don't feel guilty for doing so; that is just the devil's trick to make you persist in the sin. By cutting of all ties, you would have only done the right thing because discussions will only make it more difficult to leave the relationship. If there is no chance of marriage, then the best thing for both of you to do is cut of all contact.

Discard all the gifts you received from them. Get rid of anything that will trigger memories of the relationship. You don't need any reminders of the person; it will only make it more difficult to move on. Delete all messages, photos and any memories that you have of them. Change your phone number if it helps.

Stay away from anything that will make you miss them. Don't turn to soppy songs or movies. In fact, stay away from watching romantic movies and listening to romantic songs altogether. They will only make it harder for you to break free.

Avoid the places where you would spend time together, if avoidable, and lower your gaze if you do see them. If you can't help but check them up on their social media, then stay away from it entirely. Don't enquire others about what they are up to. This will give out the wrong signal to them and before you know it, they might be tempting you to get back together. And be on your guard not to fall for emotional blackmail.

If you've got spare time, fill it. Develop a hobby, do some volunteer work, pack your time by doing more good deeds, and whatever you can to get your mind off them. Purify yourself inwardly and outwardly.

Dear reader, never regret the incredible action that you've taken of giving up this major sin. Your ex may try to make you jealous by making you feel that you're "missing out". Don't ever let them win. Don't torture yourself with the 'what ifs'. You couldn't have done anything better than this. So stay strong.

Finally, my dear brother/sister, please do not say no to someone because of that one person you merely wish and dream will come to your house. Many people put their precious lives on hold waiting for the person to come knocking at their door and regrettably refuse many good proposals that come by for them. If they haven't done it already, then don't hold your breath and waste another moment of your life on it. Make *du'a* and *istikhaarah* and consider the incoming proposals seriously.

Turn to Allah

The most important step that you can take is turning to Allah.

Take this time to get closer to Allah. Read and ponder over the Qur'an, memorise from it, listen to some lectures, make the intention to increase your modesty in thoughts, speech and actions.

Allah is with the broken-hearted. So cry to Allah all you want, and ask Him to make things easy for you. Pour your heart out to Him. Feel the pain and let it all out. There is no better listener, nor comforter than Allah.

And when My servants ask you concerning Me - indeed I am near. I respond to the invocation of the supplicant when he calls upon Me.

(Qur'an, 2: 186)

Make sincere *du'a* (supplication), asking him to make a way out for you and to protect you from this relationship and the *fitnah* that comes along with it.

Be constant in your *tawbah* (repentance). Everyone makes mistakes, but piety lies in turning to Allah soon after. Consider the pain to be a release of your sins and seek His protection from the evil from among His creation.

Those around you may go out of their way to even remind you of the most regretful moments of your life, taunting you for your past mistakes. That is how humans are. But when you confide in Allah, you won't feel ashamed or have any regrets. People may never forgive you, but Allah will. Don't worry about what people will think, but pay heed to what Allah will think of you.

As soon as you have negative thoughts, stop them immediately by seeking refuge in Allah (through reciting your *adkhaar* and *surahs* like Surah al-Falaq and Surah an-Naas) and praying to Him. Make positive changes to your life. Your life is going to be played back to you, so make it a worthwhile watch. Submit to Allah and return to Him completely.

Chapter 6

THE AFTERMATH

Once your relationship comes to an end, you would face a whirlwind of emotions – grief, shock, denial, anger, resentment, and depression, to name a few. You need to be patient with yourself, to accept what happened, learn from it and then move on.

Everyone heals differently and at different paces. So give yourself the time you need. Realise that it may take a long time to forget (perhaps you may never forget) about this person, but that neither means that you will forever have such strong feelings for them, nor does it mean that you wouldn't be ever happy without them.

Healing doesn't mean that you no longer have emotions tied to a memory; healing occurs when you have accepted the situation as just a memory, and have learnt to be at peace with the past and yourself.

Pray for strength, forgiveness and guidance from Allah. He will surely make it easy for you.

Dealing with Heartbreak

Allah, may He be exalted says:

"Or think you that you will enter Paradise without such (trials) as came to those who passed away before you? They were afflicted with

severe poverty and ailments and were so shaken that even the Messenger and those who believed along with him said, 'When (will come) the Help of Allah?' Yes! Certainly, the Help of Allah is near!"

(Qur'an, 2: 214)

The above verse is a powerful one. It shouldn't leave any doubt in your mind that Allah certainly knows what is good for you. What you know and what you think you know is absolutely nothing compared to Allah's vast knowledge.

Shaytaan would come to you with a hundred reasons as to why it should have worked out between your ex and you. He will put doubts in your mind about leaving the *haraam* relationship for good. And in case you were the one who was dumped, then he would insinuate you with thoughts as to why things didn't work out and make you obsess over how they would have been the perfect person for you. But you have to remind yourself that Allah always knows what's best. Just because a person *seems* perfect for you, doesn't mean that they really are. People change, things happen, *life* happens. How many people who thought they were in love have ended up hating each other? Perhaps you were rescued from going through a nightmarish experience at the end of which you would be left with nothing but regret. Perhaps this was the safety net that saved you. So don't dwell on what could have been. Instead, accept Allah's Qadr, and use this opportunity to find your closure in this *haraam* relationship.

If something were written for you, then it *will* be yours, and no one can stop you from getting it. And if it were not meant to be yours, then no matter what you did to attain it, you would never be able to make it yours.

Do not accept whatever excuse Shaytaan gives you to hang onto a *haraam* relationship. Don't ever regret the *halaal* actions and decisions you took by breaking away. And always remember: you don't need to indulge in the *haraam* in order to attain the *halaal*.

In a previous chapter I had likened being 'in love' with drug addiction. Studies show that people in their initial stages of love, while looking at a picture of their loved one, have the same areas in their brain light up as those people high on cocaine. This is a great example which proves that just because one feels that they are in love doesn't necessarily mean they really are. Just as a drug user isn't in love with the drug itself, but are in love with the ecstasy they experience when taking that drug, so too are those 'in love' not so much in love with the person itself but with the *idea* of being in love and with the emotions that the lover elicits in them.

Likewise, just as an addict that tries to break away from drugs encounters withdrawal symptoms, so too would the person hooked onto love when they break free. As such, this can be a very testing time.

It may sound like a cliché but the truth is that with time you *will* heal *In Sha Allah* (Allah Willing). But this will happen only by accepting Allah's Will, by being patient with yourself, allowing yourself to feel the pain, getting closer to Allah through worship and constant prayers, beseeching Him to make it easy for you and to give you the best now and in the future.

Every ending has a new beginning. So be optimistic. Keep an open mind. And if you didn't already, then do things the *halaal* way, the right way now.

Tips on dealing with heartbreak and pain

- ✓ Social support lowers pain. So surround yourself will family and friends. Do not isolate yourself.

- ✓ Deal with the pain straight away. Don't delay it and prolong the pain.

- ✓ Get closer to Allah now. Cry to Him now. Turn to Him now. Do not numb your heart.

- ✓ Stay in the company of those that remind you of Allah.

- ✓ Don't let your suffering become a barrier between you and Allah.

- ✓ Don't look at this trial as a punishment, but as a calling from your Lord.

- ✓ Redirect your focus from the one who left you to the One who wouldn't ever –Allah.

- ✓ Trust that Allah will heal you. Bear with patience and prayer.

- ✓ Remember that the pain you are feeling is temporary, just like everything else in this world. And like everything else, it too shall pass.

- ✓ Don't complain or question, instead accept the Qadr (Will) of Allah.

- ✓ Remind yourself of your purpose in this life.

- ✓ Be grateful for everything you have. 'If you were to count the blessings of Allah never will you be able to count them.' So cheer up; you have got so much to be thankful for.

Why do I Keep Going Back?

Sometimes, when a person is not happy after ending a relationship they tend to go back to the relationship because they expect something different the second time around. What they fail to realise is that we can't expect a different outcome when repeating the same mistake.

Shaytaan might trick you into believing that you have to be with just one guy for life. This is why even if you are unhappy, you find yourself going back to him. But think about this: isn't divorce permitted in Islam? It most certainly is – and this is in case of marriage; then what about for those not even married?! This in itself is a clear indication that you don't need to be with one person for life – especially if you are not even married to them. I understand it can be hard especially if you've only seen yourself to be with one particular guy, and the guilt of 'separation' can be overwhelming, but it is a trick of the Shaytaan to keep you trapped in this doomed relationship. Beware of his ploys.

It could also be that you miss the person. You think that you need them just because you can't stop thinking about them. Take a step back from your current emotional and vulnerable state, and ask yourself what could you possibly be missing? Is it the lies, the cheating, the betrayal, the heartaches, or the headaches? Those strong feelings that you have for this person – which could be even more so when they are right before your eyes – is nothing but a pull from Shaytaan that is making you believe that this person is what you need, when it is anything but.

It happens all the time, unfortunately. Many just keep going around in circles and when they've wasted years of their time they finally get it – that it's never going to work because it was never meant to. Pure love can bring hearts that are meant to be together but lust, sin and *haraam* actions will only destroy whatever chance you had to make it work.

People need to have honest and uncomfortable conversations with themselves. They need to face themselves head-on instead of running away. It will give you a deeper understanding of why you do what you do, why you keep falling into the same old patterns. You need to face the truth, which may possibly unsettle you and shock you. But the key to contentment is getting to know yourself. It is only then that you will have control of your own life and self.

I believe this is why it's so important to allow yourself to feel the wave of emotions, and get it all over with straightaway.

82

The more you try to avoid the issues you really need to deal with, the sooner they will catch up with you to haunt you. So, deal with things head-on, no matter how much it hurts. Take it all out of your system. And then – once it's out – you are on your way to recovery.

Have deep and meaningful conversations with yourself to face your truth. And share it with God alone. At the end of the day, there is only one true place where your secrets will stay safe and this is with Allah, The Almighty. He will forgive you if you sincerely repent, unlike others in this world. That's the most beautiful thing about our faith; no matter what happens Allah is willing to accept us like no one else, love us like no one else and take us back when no one else would.

So don't secretly hope to be back with the person. Instead, cut all strings with them. If they are meant for you, it will happen in a *halaal* way (and *halaal* steps have to be taken to make it work). *Haraam* beginnings generally have very hurtful endings.

Take Responsibility

Humility reaps tremendous benefits. I believe that taking responsibility of the situation and forgiving yourself as well as the person who hurt you can heal your heart in many ways. Once you have broken up, it is imperative to ask yourself where you went wrong. I don't mean to say 'where you went wrong *within* the *haraam* relationship'; I mean 'where did you *primarily* go wrong'. The answer to that introspective question is this: In your disobedience to Allah.

The spiritual as well as practical dangers of getting involved in *haraam* relationships burn and scar someone just like fire does, leaving behind pain that can take a long time to recover from. So take your sin seriously. Once you do so, you will start to hate it and every memory attached to it. This will then help you recover as it will lead you to stop missing what you now wish you hadn't indulged in in the first place.

At this stage, it should be no more about you and them (your ex); it should only be about you and Allah. You see, relationships aren't just between us and another individual but they are all linked to Allah. Take for example, when we are indulged in *haraam* relationships, we are not only taking from the rights of another fellow human being, but we are also neglecting the *sunnah* (the Prophetic way), and disregarding the Laws of Allah.

When you learn to take yourself and your daily actions to account in this way, you develop *taqwa* (God-consciousness) which acts as your safety net from falling apart, and gives you every reason to smile. You will also nurture a stronger relationship with yourself and with others too. And if something goes 'wrong' in any relationship you will realise that its either one of four things: a test, the consequence of falling short in following the Qur'an or *sunnah* (which you can always learn from and try harder to improve on), or that it was something that wasn't good for you and would've caused you harm or that it was *haraam* that was to be doomed anyway.

Therefore, take it all back to Allah. Accepting responsibility of your sin, acknowledging that it was wrong, regretting it, repenting from it, sincerely making the decision not to ever be in a *haraam* relationship again, and making constant *istighfar* (repentance) will heal your broken heart.

In your pursuit to taking responsibility of your actions, you can very well cry to Allah. If you were cheated on or suffered greatly because of your ex, then complain only to Allah. Don't badmouth them, try and forgive them and if you can't do that then remember that Allah is Most Just. Fall down in *sajdah* (prostration) to Allah, relieving your pain, anxiety and heartbreak. And He will turn your pain into strength, your anxiety into peace and your broken heart into a purified one.

"Allah is the ally of those who believe. He brings them out from darknesses into the light. And those who disbelieve - their allies are Taghut. They take them out of the light into darknesses. Those are the companions of the Fire; they will abide eternally therein."

(Qur'an, 2:257)

Gratitude

Gratitude helps the heart to heal wonderfully. Once you start praising Allah and thanking Him for removing you from the *haraam* relationship – either by it ending badly wherein you had no choice in the matter, or by you taking the brave decision yourself to leave the *haraam* relationship for the sake of Allah — only then will you begin to really appreciate what has happened. Because the moment the sinful relationship stopped is the moment in which *you* stopped sinning.

SubhanAllah (Glory be to Allah), just think about this for a minute and reflect deeply. If they had cheated on you, lied to you, 'catfished' you, or whatever it was that they did to get you into the relationship, know that you aren't the loser. Instead, you have been saved — yes, saved! Through the downfall of this *haraam* relationship, you are saved from continuing a dangerous and major sin; you no longer have to deal with everyday clashes, you don't have to live in fear and desperation, going crazy in what you thought was 'love'. This event has led you one step closer to God, and a million steps further from another million sins! So my dear, do not grieve over your relationship, your past, or your heartbreak but grow from it and rejoice because you came out of a world of hell, alive and with a chance to make up for your sins by doing good, and returning to the Source of all love, Allah Al-Wadūd (The Loving One).

If you do this, then you would go a long way from where you were when you first broke up; you would feel refreshed, reenergised, and maybe even become who you used to be before you lost yourself in this *haraam* relationship. If you aren't there yet, then persevere a little more and *In Sha Allah* (Allah Willing) you will be there soon.

Don't give up on yourself. Great things come through patience, so have *sabr* (patience).

"O young man, I shall teach you some words [of advice]: Be mindful of Allah and Allah will protect you. Be mindful of Allah and you will find Him in front of you. If you ask, then ask Allah [alone]; and if you seek help, then seek help from Allah [alone]. And know that if the nation were to gather together to benefit you with anything, they would not benefit you except with what Allah had already prescribed for you. And if they were to gather together to harm you with anything, they would not harm you except with what Allah had already prescribed against you. The pens have been lifted and the pages have dried."

(It was related by at-Tirmidhi, who said it was a good and sound hadeeth.) Another narration, other than that of Tirmidhi, reads:

Be mindful of Allah, and you will find Him in front of you. Recognise and acknowledge Allah in times of ease and prosperity, and He will remember you in times of adversity. And know that what has passed you by [and you have failed to attain] was not going to befall you, and what has befallen you was not going to pass you by. And know that victory comes with patience, relief with affliction, and hardship with ease.

(40 Hadith Nawawi 19)

There is something very beautiful about pain and heartbreak – and that is the vulnerability that it brings which serves as a powerful reminder for us of the fact that we have no control over our lives; it reminds us that we are completely dependent on Allah. Perhaps this is why pain is essential, because it builds our faith and grows our character. It instils within us characteristics like wisdom and empathy that enable us to become better human beings, draw closer to our Creator and provide a support system for those who need it the most. Pain can prepare us in ways that we didn't think was possible. I believe this is the hidden beauty in pain.

Therefore don't be sad for what befalls you of calamities. Instead, look for the positive in every situation, and your heart will be content.

Your love of Allah is your shield against heartbreak; make it the strongest and the biggest love of your life. It is the only love that will never leave you. It's the only love that will last forever; the only love that won't hurt; and the only love that will become your strength.

When you have got so much love to give, give it to Allah – the One who is always going to be there. When your heart is with Allah, it can never be really broken, as Ash-Shāfi the Healer will keep it safe.

You were created to worship Allah. So don't share the level of love and dependency you need to have on Him with anyone else in this world.

And (yet), among the people are those who take other than Allah as equals (to Him). They love them as they (should) love Allah. But those who believe are stronger in love for Allah.

(Qur'an, 2:165)

Now, I don't mean to say that you should withhold love from those who are lawful for you to love. What I mean is simply that you shouldn't *depend* on this love. Love (and don't hold back that love) but do not ever equate it to the love you should only feel for Allah – the highest form of love, the type of love that makes you think, feel or say, "I can't live without them." Don't place and expect all your happiness in the love of another human being. Don't let anyone take you away from Allah.

Instead, take some time out, get to know yourself, get to know Allah, and surround yourself with His reminders by reading the Qur'an, and doing a lot of *dhikr* with understanding. *Subhanallah* (Glory be to Allah), it is an amazing experience that gives life to the lifeless heart, and acts as a medicine for the soul. Make a commitment to performing *salah* (prayer) on time. Dress and behave modestly. Try to stay in a state of purity as much in the day as you can. Stop listening to music and watching romantic movies.

In short, make the most of your time in developing yourself as well as your relationship with your Maker. Listen to Islamic lectures, read Islamic books by reliable sources, pray to Allah, ask Him to forgive you, and have hope that He, Al-Ghafūr (the Forgiving One) will forgive. It is important that you believe Allah loves you and will forgive you so you are able to love and forgive yourself. Don't let Shaytaan trick you into believing otherwise; he would wish that you despair of Allah's Mercy just so you stay stuck in this rut.

Heartbreak can be a huge blessing if we let it be. It's a way of purification for the one who comes closer to Allah because of it, but a curse for the one who is taken farther away from Him because of it.

So fall completely in love with Allah, and prioritise that love, where no other love can compete with it so that you are free of need and sorrow. For it is in this love that your heart will find relief.

Always remember why you were created. Always remember your purpose so it pulls your heart and head out of the cloud of *dunya* and into reality. This will help you to recover from any hardship you are going through because you will be able to see the bigger picture – your purpose.

"Did you think that We had created you in play (without any purpose), and that you would not be brought back to Us?" So Exalted be Allah, the True King: Laa ilaaha illa Huwa (none has the right to be worshipped but He), the Lord of the Supreme Throne!"
(Qur'an, 23:115 – 116)

"We created not the heavens and the earth and all that is between them for a (mere) play"
(Qur'an, 21:16)

We created them not except with truth (i.e. to examine and test those who are obedient and those who are disobedient and then reward the obedient ones and punish the disobedient ones), but most of them know not"
(Qur'an, 44:38)

"Who has created death and life that He may test you which of you is best in deed. And He is the All-Mighty, the Oft-Forgiving"
(Qur'an, 67:2)

"And I (Allah) created not the jinn and mankind except that they should worship Me (Alone)"
(Qur'an, 51:56)

Chapter 7

BEYOND THE BOOK

Do I Have to Confess...?

Do I have to confess my sin to my fiancé, future husband, or others?

If a person has repented for their sins and turned a new leaf, it is wrong to question them about it. Neither does your fiancé (or husband) have the right to ask you about your past sins, nor are you, as a (potential) spouse, obliged to inform them of it – especially if Allah has concealed it for you.

If Allah has concealed your sin, then you should not publicise it, as the Prophet (peace and blessings be upon him) said:

"Avoid filth that Allah has forbidden. Whoever does any such thing, let him conceal it with the concealment of Allah."

(Bayhaqi; authentic)

This is a very private sin that should only stay between you and Allah. Don't ever bring it up, and don't ever ask your spouse of their past either. You are not meant to live in the past. So if you do bring it up, then it may very well hinder you from moving on happily with your future.

Is Love that Ends in Marriage Allowed?

There are many cases of couples who date before they end up getting married. What is the ruling for such cases? Is it allowed?

The *haraam* acts that precede a marriage are clearly sinful. However the marriage itself, if concluded correctly and with the consent of the guardian, is valid.

However, I must add in the same breath that it is important for both spouses to repent for the *haraam* they engaged in before making it *halaal*. Moreover, as we have expounded earlier in the book, dating is not justified with the intention of marriage.

How do Some *Haraam* Relationships End in Marriage and Others in Destruction?

I have been asked this question a couple of times now – "Why did my (*haraam*) relationship end terribly, while others ended in happy marriages? I feel envious of my friends that are marrying their boyfriends!"

I don't have all the answers and I'm not going to pretend that I do. But what I will do is give an example of real situations that I know about and hope that it would give you a clearer perspective of things:

Case 1: A lovely girl from a lovely family fell into the terrible sin of engaging in a forbidden relationship. She avoided the *haraam* all her life, staying away from it as best she could but this time, she had slipped. Anyways, she suffered mental abuse and torture and it was very difficult for her to leave the relationship because he wouldn't let her. The whole thing ended badly causing her years of emotional turmoil.

Case 2: Another girl who wasn't very religious and had a bit of a 'reputation' in the community didn't see *haraam* relationships as a problem; she found it to be a casual thing, "no big deal". She ended up marrying her boyfriend, whom she now lives happily with, along with their kids.

However, if we scrutinised this girl's background, we'd find that she came from a dysfunctional family. Her mother had issues, to put it kindly and her dad had left them. She didn't have a normal or a happy family life.

But the former girl did.

So one girl had a happy family background, and her *haraam* relationship ended badly. And another girl had her *haraam* relationship turn into a marriage, while she had a problematic family background.

My point is that you shouldn't be envious of anyone, assuming that they are more blessed than you, or believing that something is wrong with you for it not to have worked out or developed into marriage. Everyone has tests in life which they have to face. Moreover, we need to realise that just because the girl married her boyfriend, doesn't mean that everything is fine and dandy, and that the sin doesn't count. It most certainly does count, and they will be recompensed for it by Allah in this world and the next –

unless they sincerely repent. So for this girl, even though her marriage is a happy one, it is also an added test.

There are yet other cases wherein people get married to the person they've been dating, but their marriage doesn't last long.

So please don't envy anyone or dwell on why things didn't work out the way you wanted them to. Instead, count your blessings; you ended up with someone who wasn't good for you, so Allah removed them from your life and saved you from continuing your sin. Thank and praise Him.

Here is my final note on this topic: Studies have shown that *most* marriages that are based on prior love between a man and woman fail, whereas most that are not based on *haraam* relationships – commonly known as "traditional marriages", succeed.

A field study done by a French sociologist concluded that marriage is more likely to succeed when the two parties did not fall in love before marriage. Another study undertaken by Professor Isma'eel Abd Al-Baari of 1,500 families concluded that more than 75% of love marriages ended in divorce, whilst the rate among traditional marriages, those which were not based on prior love was less than 5%.

Resisting Sexual Desires

Sexual desire is normal for human beings. However, we are required to refrain from expressing it in forbidden ways, and only do so in ways that our Maker has permitted.

We must protect ourselves by reducing and weakening the things that may provoke desire within us.

This can be done by lowering the gaze, which unfortunately isn't always easy to do, but can be made easy with some will-power and practise *In Sha Allah* (Allah Willing).

"And tell the believing women to lower their gaze (from looking at forbidden things), and protect their private parts (from illegal sexual acts)"

(Qur'an, 24: 31)

The Prophet (peace and blessings of Allah be upon him) said:

"Do not follow one glance with another, for the first is allowed but not the second."

(Tirmidhi, Hadith 2701; authentic)

Therefore, lowering the gaze definitely does help one resist sexual desires and should be taken seriously.

One should avoid romantic novels and movies, especially those with sexual content. Unfortunately, a lot of TV contains sexual references; so if you can't totally switch it off, then look away, mute and forward it. Refrain from internet sites that make it even more difficult for you to lower you gaze.

Abstaining from bad company is a must. If you are around those who talk about dating or forbidden relationships all the time, or make constant references to it, then this will only make things more difficult. Avoid mingling with the opposite sex. Set boundaries for yourself.

Keep your mind healthily occupied. If you have too much free time on your hands, it may lead to your mind wandering. As they say, "An idle mind is the devil's workshop."

A strong relationship with Allah strengthens the heart and soul. You are less likely to give into temptation if you have *taqwa* (God-consciousness) of Allah, and you spend your time in doing good deeds and abstaining from evil as well as the paths that lead to evil.

Fasting is yet another method to control sexual desires, as the Prophet (peace and blessings of Allah be upon him) said:

"O young men, whoever among you can afford to, let him get married, for it is more effective in lowering the gaze and in guarding one's chastity. Whoever cannot afford it, then let him fast, for it will be a shield for him." This is addressed to young men, but it also includes young women."

(Sunan al-Nasa'i, Book 26, Hadith 14; authentic)

We must also educate ourselves about the righteous men and women who have guarded their chastity such as Maryam and Prophet Yusuf (may Allah be pleased with them). There is much to benefit from these noble slaves of Allah.

"And Maryam (Mary), the daughter of 'Imraan, who guarded her chastity. And We breathed into (the sleeve of her shirt or her garment) through Our Rooh [i.e. Jibreel (Gabriel)], and she testified to the truth of the Words of her Lord [i.e. believed in the Words of Allah:

"Be!" and he was; that is 'Eesa (Jesus), son of Maryam (Mary) as a Messenger of Allah], and (also believed in) His Scriptures, and she was of the Qaanitoon (i.e. obedient to Allah)"

(Qur'an, 66: 12)

"He said: 'O my Lord! Prison is dearer to me than that to which they invite me (i.e. illicit relations). Unless You turn away their plot from me, I will feel inclined towards them and be one (of those who commit sin and deserve blame or those who do deeds) of the ignorant'

So his Lord answered his invocation and turned away from him their plot. Verily, He is the All-Hearer, the All-Knower"

(Qur'an, 12: 33)

"Verily, the Muslims (those who submit to Allah in Islam) men and women, the believers men and women (who believe in Islamic Monotheism),…the men and the women who guard their chastity (from illegal sexual acts) and the men and the women who remember Allah much with their hearts and tongues. Allah has prepared for them forgiveness and a great reward (i.e. Paradise"

(Qur'an, 33: 35)

Once you realise the magnitude and dangers of *haraam* relationships and unlawful sexual relations, your heart will automatically turn away from it *In Sha Allah*. You know yourself better than anyone else, so examine what your weaknesses are, where you are most vulnerable, and tackle them in order to guard yourself.

Put Allah first, fear Allah's judgement and not the judgement of people.

97

Finally, marriage is a true blessing. It protects one from the *haraam*, and helps you fulfil your natural desires in a permissible way as the Prophet (peace and blessings of Allah be upon him) said:

"O young men, whoever among you can afford it, let him get married, for it is more effective in lowering the gaze and guarding one's chastity. And whoever cannot afford it should fast, for it will be a shield for him."

(Sunan al-Nasa'i, Book 26, Hadith 14; authentic)

So if you are able to, then get married.

Seeking Marriage

Do not let your pain and past come between your happiness and future. If people come to you for your hand and you are pleased with the proposal then please seriously consider it.

I'm not advising you to jump straight into marriage, no. Sometimes the hurtful memories can stay with us for years, but that is normal as long as you don't let it control your present or your future. Don't let it get in the way of attaining the right match for you.

In this section, I would like to expound on what you need to abstain from when it comes to seeking marriage. There are plenty of books out there that detail the do's of the process, but not too many that shine light on the don'ts.

The first and foremost advice that I'd lend in this regard is not to pursue your marriage talks on your own. Too many girls get taken advantage of in this way. What might start of as *halaal* may end up in *haraam*. Remember Allah's admonition to not even go near *zina* (illicit relations), let alone commit it.

It is okay to talk to someone you are interested in with a *wali* (legal guardian), but he must be an adult who is to be involved from the onset of the relationship. I wouldn't recommend you taking say, a younger brother in his teens as a *wali* for yourself.

If you resort to talking directly to the significant other via Facebook, WhatsApp, the phone, or through meet-ups, it (most possibly) won't lead to anything serious.

If you want to show someone you are serious about marriage, involve your *wali* (preferably an older brother, or an adult like your father) right from the start. Involve the potential person's elder(s) too. This makes it clear for the both of you that this guy or girl isn't just "testing the waters", wasting your time, or is trying to entice you into a *haraam* relationship.

Many guys use marriage as a ruse to pull the girl in. Days and nights of conversations ultimately lead to meet-ups. And once they've fulfilled their agenda, they begin to rattle off excuses as to why the marriage won't work just now. By this time, the girl is too attached to the suitor and finds it very difficult to get herself out; it's almost like she's sinking deeper and deeper into quicksand, wherein she may begin compromising her morals by giving him more time, desperate to hold his attention and interest in her. This is when most girls lose themselves, and end up crossing the line that they've never dreamt of crossing. And when the girl finally does so to keep this low-life man in her life, it turns out to be the final act which pushes him to leave her. Because now she is no more respected or valued like she once was; she is 'used' and no longer needed in his eyes. If this happens to you (God forbid) then please do not repeat the cycle of abuse; you cannot make someone else a substitute to take your pain out on.

So always involve a *wali*. It is fine if you want to message as long as you add a *wali* to the conversation. And right from the get-go, even if it's the first meeting, take your *wali* with you (again, preferably someone older than you) and encourage the other person to do the same. You can always make arrangements to ensure a bit of privacy without stirring the issue of *khalwah* (seclusion) up, for instance, the two of you can sit and talk at a table different from but close to your father's.

In your talks with each other, make sure you discuss things that are most important to you, rather than whiling away time on casual topics. Prepare a list of what's important to you and be ready to ask relevant questions.

I'm not going to delve too much into the topic of marriage in this book. I'll leave this for a different book *In Sha Allah* (Allah Willing).

Chapter 8

REAL-LIFE STORIES

In this chapter, you will find real accounts of *haraam* relationships that were sent to me personally by those involved in them. From a sister who got played and betrayed, to a sister that that got possessed by a *jinni*, to another that almost lost her faith – these are stories of women that learnt the difference between love and lust the hard way, women who had their hearts shattered and trusts broken, women who struggled with their *eeman,* but also women who turned back to Allah, and rose out of their ordeal, repentant and stronger in their relationship with their Lord. Each of these women has a story to share and a message to impart for us to take benefit from.

I would like to take this opportunity to thank all the sisters who shared their very personal stories with me and with the readers of this book so that we could learn, benefit and take heed from them. May Allah forgive them and replace their bad deeds with good deeds and let this book be a shield for them against the fire. Aameen.

A wise person learns from the mistakes of others. So let's learn from their stories.

#1

I used to be involved with a guy for many years. I thought the best way to keep the relationship going was to always impress him, and make sure that I gave him all the love he desires. The fact was that in the process of this 'giving' I was losing myself. At the age of sixteen I felt really happy as he was still with me but at seventeen I felt incomplete. I was realising that this wasn't making me happy. It took me some more time to realise that I was losing interest in praying. But then Allah removed the guy from my life and I was heartbroken. They say that Allah puts you through a situation to bring you closer to him. This turning point in my life was just that.

The biggest piece of advice I can give you is that it's really not worth obsessing over a boy/girl thinking that just because others are involving themselves in such situations, you need to too. There's more to life than this. Focus on yourself and on drawing closer to Allah (*subhanahu wa ta'ala*). I have learnt my lesson and now am on the right path, *alhamdulliah*. *In Sha Allah* next year I will get married to a man I love for the sake of Allah, the *halaal* way. Real love starts only after *nikkah*.

#2

I loved a man very much. He meant the world to me. We talked every day for two years. Then over the course of our relationship, we became religious by the Grace of Allah and we realised the wrong that we were doing.

One Ramadan we decided to take a break from communicating with each other and give ourselves a chance to think about our relationship and the *haraam* that we were committing. We both then realised how much we loved each other and how badly we wanted to live together not just in the *dunya* but in Jannah as well. At the end of that Ramadan, we decided to stop talking altogether and save our love for each other in our hearts until we could get married. We followed the *hadith* "Whoever leaves something for the sake of Allah, Allah will replace it with something better" (*Musnad Ahmad, Hadith 22565; authentic*) to a T and here we are now. It has been two years and our life has changed so much since then – all for the better.

Alhamdulillah (all praise is due to Allah) for guiding us to the right path.

#3

It all started in college. He sat next to me. I was a young and naive girl back then. He asked me my name, and my general whereabouts. It was a typical American encounter that made us find out that we were of the same religion, ethnicity, and culture. What a coincidence! The first (rather fairy-tale-like) thought that came to mind was this: *Potential life partner?*

He started off being nice, sweet, and everything that one can describe a stranger with motives as being. We exchanged our phone numbers but only for the purpose of studying and keeping up with the course through group work – although this was something that my father had strictly forbidden me

103

from doing, i.e. interacting with the opposite sex even if it were for study. I didn't think much of it since we were talking only for the purposes of school and nothing else. But just after a short while, it turned into something much more serious when he decided to ask me out. Hesitant, I told him that I didn't date, but that if we were to talk of such matter, it would only be for getting to know each other for the purpose of marriage in the future. He worked his charm and told me that he wanted to get to know me for no reason other than that, and even claimed that he could already picture me as his wife.

Days, weeks, months, and a year went by of countless talks, texts, and in-person hangouts. We met up at the school, library, cafeteria, malls, parks, and pretty much everywhere we could. He always made time for me, showing me around different places, putting in a lot of effort to make all our outings pleasurable and fun. And he spoke to me with such charm and wit that I ultimately fell in love with him. He would always remind me of how nice it would be for us to be married to each other, and how nice it would be to have both families together. I was a family-oriented girl, so his talks of family made me fall all the more in love with him.

As time passed, he started to get more physical with me. It began with a kiss on the lips, and when I fought back he would remind me, "You are mine, and will always be mine. Now, can I get a kiss from my future wife?" I believed in his words, and gave in to it. A kiss led to an inappropriate touch, which further transgressed to much more – *zina!* Soon after, I felt extremely guilty and anxious at the thought of getting caught by my parents and friends. I knew what I was doing was wrong, but at the same time did not want to upset this boy who had promised me marriage and more. I would counter my guilt with thoughts like, "It's okay; we will get married in the future anyway." I would relieve myself of the constant guilt this way, and continued to do anything that made him happy. He must have sensed that I was not feeling as comfortable as before, so in order to overcome this problem, he bought me a 'promise ring' – a symbol intended to convince me of his loyalty. With this ring, I of course, only got another reason to be with him and believe in his words.

Time passed by and I noticed that he was beginning to act suspicious and rude, treating me with very little respect. Every time I confronted him about his changed ways, he would blame *me* for it. This new side of him came out right before my eyes. I was not happy with him, but did not want to leave him for what we had been through. My constant question to myself was: 'Who else would want to marry me after I have been kissed, touched, and used inappropriately?'

One day as I secretly went through his private messages, one of my worst fears came true; he was engaged to another girl from their homeland. The only excuse he came up with was that it was just a joke and that he really was not engaged. This led to suspicion and constant fights. He finally came forth to tell me that his parents had forced him into this engagement since he was a little kid. Lies were followed with more lies. But I did not fight or seek out revenge. I bottled my emotions up, and cried frequently – not at the loss of the cheating boy, but at the thought of the sins I've committed, and worst of all, the *zina* (may Allah forgive me). I finally turned to Allah. With the help of the internet and social media, I began to read and research on the process of repentance, and implemented it as much as I could.

"Verily with hardship comes ease." With the help of my family, I met the man of my dreams, *alhamdulillah*. Even though I didn't reveal to him my past sins and *zina*, my new fiancé slowly but surely found out about it. However, this man was able to move forward – as hard as it was – and accepted me for the true love, pure heart, and good intentions he saw inside of me.

I am now a practicing Muslim, praying five times a day, fasting during the month of Ramadan, and repenting to Allah with every *du'a* (supplication) I make. I will forever repent in every prayer, and every day for the rest of my life. *Zina* should not be taken lightly; it comes with harsh punishment in this *dunya* and on the Day of Judgment.

My sincere advice to every girl is this: Unless a boy seeks either his parents', or your parents' approval for your hand in marriage, do not move forward with this so-called "relationship". Unfortunately, many girls fall for lust, words of promise, and thoughts of encountering 'love' before marriage and give in easily. Unless it is done the Islamic way, it is not worth the time, effort, dignity, and respect. No matter how hard it may be, no matter how honest a boy may be to you, unless it is the Islamic way, leave it. There is hope as long as you put your trust in Allah and vow to proceed in life with good intentions and good deeds.

I truly hope this helps any girl out there, who is going through a *haraam* relationship, or a girl who has come out from a *haraam* relationship, or a girl who has gone through this exact experience. Please abandon the *haraam* relationship.

Allah says in the Qur'an:

"Say: 'O my Servants who have transgressed against their souls! Despair not of the Mercy of Allah: for Allah forgives all sins: for He is Oft-Forgiving, Most Merciful.'"

(Qur'an, 39: 53)

"Allah accepts the repentance of those who do evil in ignorance and repent soon afterwards; to them will Allah turn in mercy: For Allah is full of knowledge and wisdom."

(Qur'an, 4: 17)

I met a guy about four years ago. He was actually a childhood friend but we had lost contact with each other somewhere along the way. When we reunited years later, he seemed like a dream come true with every word he said, and everything he did for me. After several rejections of his proposal, I finally decided to pursue a relationship with him because he had won me over. But that was when my downfall began.

He would make me feel insecure by constantly bragging about his past *haraam* relationships which in turn made me feel as though I needed to be like that too. Shaytaan played his games with my mind, and I began dressing revealingly. I even began missing prayers the days I went to see him. I would say and do anything for this guy just to please him.

Although this story may sound typical, it was anything but. One day I dreamt a scary-looking girl saying the guy's name (and hers) telling me to leave him because "he was hers". I didn't pay much attention to the dream until the day I received a call on private with the voice of the same girl that said the same things as in my dream. It made me shiver and from that day onwards, I felt something inside of me hurt and make me cry every night. It was an indescribable feeling.

When I mentioned the girl's name and asked him if he knew her, he looked shocked and scared. He revealed that that was the name of his ex-girlfriend, and wondered how I knew about her. He went on to explain that she had tried to perform black magic on him and that things got really bad at one point in time.

In my dreaded dream, the girl had promised me that she would take me away from my *deen,* and make me come so close to him that it would eventually leave me crazy. And that's exactly what happened. I became near-suicidal. I was extremely attached to him – to a point where I became 'crazy', partaking in *haraam* activities with him just so he wouldn't leave me. He became a minster in my life. Even though he treated me badly, I felt as if I couldn't leave him.

I soon started getting attacked from within myself by a *jinni,* and that's when I thought I've had enough. I had to do something about it. I told my family about him and asked them for help. After having *ruqyah* (Prophetic healing) done on myself, we found out that I was possessed by a *jinn* sent by his ex-girlfriend. When I informed the guy of this, he backed out completely and started acting like he didn't want to do anything with me anymore.

Leaving the guy was hard, but turning back to my *deen* was harder. I slowly learnt to place my trust in Allah and at the start of Ramadan I not only left him but started wearing the *hijab* too. I repented every single night and asked Allah to guide me, and *alhamdulliah* I have never been happier. I feel like Allah has given me another chance in life and *In Sha Allah,* I will never go back to how I used to be.

#5

My cousin, three months younger than me, and I were the best of friends when we were little. Around the age of six or seven years, they moved to another country. But there was gossip within the whole family that we'd be together when we got older. Not everyone would talk about it but a distant relative would say something that made me think about him in a completely different way. Once a friend in school told me that my mom told her mom something along the lines of me and my cousin set to be together. To this day, I don't know if it was true or not. But my innocence as a little girl, the constant teasing by friends in school, and the talks of relatives, altogether made me believe that I was totally in love with him. Teenage years are like that – when one thinks, rather believes that they are 'in love' and would do everything to be with their loved one. I even thought to confess my undying love to him. But deep down, I knew that what I felt was not real love; it was just a result of people's talks that got to me.

Once when I was in my late teens I read a novel by a famous writer and it made me think of what I was actually doing to myself; I was losing my *eeman* for something *haraam*. I remember it was a Friday morning and everyone was asleep (I guess it was Ramadan). I felt a strong urge to recite Surah Al-Kahf slowly and peacefully, and to understand every word. So I put on Qari Mishary Rashid's recitation and started reciting along. I cried profusely and asked Allah to help me get out of the mess I'd gotten myself into. I felt so dirty and bad. But *alhamdulillah* Allah answered my prayer.

I started maintaining a distance from my cousin and started covering properly (not just in front of him but every other *non-mahram* as well) and tried to follow what Islam says. I admit that it wasn't easy at all. There were moments when I thought that I couldn't do this and I needed my dose of reverie of the imaginary life I'd made up in which he played an important part. But Allah helped me and *alhamdulillah* I'm a very proud Muslimah now. My uncle's family comes and goes, but it does not affect me in any emotional way.

I've started believing that if Allah has set me with someone then I will definitely be with him *In Sha Allah*. So why should I dirty my thoughts by fantasising about a *non-mahram*, when it would also be a form of injustice for my future spouse. I considered it to be like a betrayal made against him. *Alhamdulillah* for Allah's guidance.

I just wish to tell every boy and girl out there: Please do not let Shaytaan play a major role in your lives. We should satisfy Allah instead of Shaytaan, and believe that Allah has something in store for all of us. After all, Allah is with those who have patience. So all we need to do is be patient, and Allah will give us an unexpected and beautiful reward.

#6

I am a Muslim but my doubts about my faith began the moment I fell in love with a Christian. We started off as course mates. Although I gave him the cold shoulder at first,

I opened up to him as a friend later. As time passed, we developed feelings for each other and I didn't realise then that I was actually getting myself caught in the trap of Shaytaan.

The guy would talk to me about the future, and tell how he wanted me to start a family with him. As a girl, obviously when a guy talks to you about how you will travel the world and pray together, you immediately 'fall in love' and begin daydreaming. That is what happened with me. Our relationship continued but with lots of arguments about conversion. He bought me a Bible which I accepted without complaining. He was so good with religious arguments; it scared me because when I brought up anything about Islam, he would counter immediately and convincingly, leaving me dumbfounded. I told him that I loved and believed in the original message of Jesus Christ (may Allah be pleased with him), but he wanted me to accept him as my Lord and Saviour.

I wanted to keep this guy; I didn't want to lose him so I stopped praying, I stopped going for *Jumu'ah* (Friday prayers) and reading the Qur'an. I wanted to keep our endless hangouts and night calls going. What I was doing unknowingly was losing my identity to be loved in return. Many of my female friends noticed this and they advised me against it but I did not listen. I recall the day I attended a Christian marriage seminar with him; before I entered, a Muslim brother had implored me not to go for the sake of Allah, but I had said that I couldn't break my promise to my boyfriend. While I was there my mind was at the call of prayer. I heard but did not obey.

This distance between myself and Allah took a toll on me. I was depressed, anxious and worried all the time. I will never forget the two nights when my boyfriend told me that he was getting frustrated at me because of this issue on conversion. I saw another person, entirely someone different in him. He always found faults in me, hurting me with painful words. I would cry then, but I always respected his feelings no matter how angry I was. Imagine a guy telling you to your face that he deleted your number out of annoyance. It made me sad – devastated even.

He eventually asked me if I could give my religion up for a relationship with him. I knew my answer will be 'no' but also knew what its implication would be. As expected, he got angry at me. I asked him, "Must I strip off my identity to be with you?" for which he replied, "You must because if you don't, I will make it to Heaven but you won't since you did not accept Christianity." He told me that I either knew the truth but refused to accept, or was simply being selfish. I felt condemned not by God but by a guy.

That ended things between us. *Alhamdulillah* for the guidance of Allah; Even though I considered giving up Islam – my Islam – to be with him, deep down I still held on to Allah not wanting to let my desires control me. I transgressed from the path of Islam once when I 'fell in love' with him; I wasn't going to sacrifice all of my Islam for him.

When I think back to it all, I realise that I was pressured into commitment. But what good did that bring me? I know he has moved on; and even though I have let go I still cry sometimes remembering the bond we once shared. He made me realise and understand many things but I wish that I had told him about the truth – Islam.

Moving on from someone one was attached to is difficult – but with every hardship comes ease. I now carry my loneliness with a smile and a resolve: even though I couldn't make an impact on one person, I can try to impact others that I come across in my life by doing my best to obliterate the misconceptions people have about Islam. I pray that people see the truth of Islam and accept it as the only peaceful way of life.

***

Most *haraam* relationships end in hate. Nothing but grief, sorrow and regret comes from engaging in such a relationship.

There are countless other stories like these – stories that tell of the horrors faced by people who have experienced the forbidden relationship.

Pay heed and make a conscious decision not to sacrifice your mental health, physical health, and most of all, your faith in the name of 'love'.

Chapter 9

QUOTES

Boonaa Mohammed

Haraam relationships usually don't have *halaal* endings.

Dr Bilal Philips

Don't stay in a *haraam* relationship with the intention of making it *halaal* someday. Who promised you tomorrow?

You're worth more than being someone's girlfriend or boyfriend. Either you're married or you're not. Don't glorify *haraam* relationships.

What is *haraam*, will always be *haraam*, even if the whole world engages in it.

Imagine the person you're in a *haraam* relationship with will talk against you on the day of judgement. Get married.

Love someone for the sake of Allah, Allah will make it last forever; leave someone for the sake of Allah, Allah will give you someone better.

Shaykh Hasan Ali

If you find sweetness in *haraam*, Allah will take the sweetness away from the *halaal*.

115

Shaykh Yasir Qadhi

Falling in love isn't *haraam;* it's what you do with that love that makes it *haraam* or *halaal.*

Shaykh Yassir Fazaga

The word 'love' in the Qur'an appears in over 90 places, but interestingly, it doesn't define the word 'love', but speaks about the very first consequence of love - commitment. Islam talks about commitment. If you truly love something or someone, you commit. If you don't, then your claim of 'real love' is not real at all.

Sheikh Khalid Yasin

Haraam relationship and *zina* can lead you to the Hell-Fire but *halaal* relationship and *nikkah* can complete half your *eemaan* and can lead you to Paradise.

Haraam relationships will never bring peace to your heart.

Unknown

Haraam love is just like salty water. No matter how much you drink from it, it will never quench your thirst, it will increase it.

They lied to you when they told that 'true love hurts'. True love never hurts because it is granted by the Controller of the hearts: Allah. True love is a blessing from Him because it comes after marriage; blessings would never hurt a believer but love inspired by Shaytaan will surely hurt you. The little heart beating in your chest is so precious so keep it for your husband or wife.

The greatest problem a lot of the unmarried Muslims face are non-*halaal* relationship issues. The easiest way to overcome this problem is simple. Put Allah first. When you make Allah your priority, He will bless you with the right people in the right time. Trust Allah with your situation. Know that He has your whole life under control. There's no point stressing or running after anyone. What's *naseeb* is written.

When one leaves a *haraam* relationship or a sin for Allah, He will give them better, take away the love of that sin, and grant sweetest of *eeman*.

Halaal is a must; not just about what we eat, but also about what we hear and what we love.

Leave him, and if he is truly yours then you will have him in a *halaal* manner eventually.

We sin as if He is seeing nothing.

Walk away for the sake of the one who created you and He will guide you to the one who is meant for you. Walk away from *haraam* relationships.

Halaal is the only definition of love.

Women are gifts from Allah to men. Don't be reckless with a woman's heart. Be honest and sincere and follow your intentions with your actions. Remember, you will be a father one day. Would you stand and watch if someone played with your daughter and deceived her? And sisters, if a brother shows interest in you and isn't willing to commit to you with marriage, then forget about him.

If you consider a woman less pure after you've touched her, then maybe you should take a look at your hands.

A real man looks for a wife – not another girlfriend.

The difference between a girlfriend and wife: A wife completes your *deen*. A girlfriend destroys whatever *deen* you have.

The girl usually supports her brother when he is in love. But the boy never supports his sister if she's in love because even though she knows the meaning of love, he knows the nature of a man's intentions.

If it was good, it would've stayed

QUOTES
BY MARYAM YOUSAF

The Queen

The way he looks at you melts your heart. The way he chases after you, ready to do anything; The way he calls you, first thing in the morning and last thing at night. The way he makes you feel as if you're the most beautiful girl alive. The way he treats you like a queen, just the way he treats all his other girlfriends you have not yet seen. Men will do whatever they can just to get your attention but it takes a real man to keep it; a real man to make you his wife and the queen of his house.

Let Go

Letting go of *haraam* relationships might be hard but what is harder is holding onto something that isn't yours. Let it go.

Don't Cry

I've witnessed people cry over the things that they loved but never attained for years. I've also witnessed the same people, when finally acquiring what they thought they couldn't live without, turn away from what they were granted because they realised it wasn't what they wanted after all. So don't cry but always be grateful for what you do and don't have.

Praying

What if they will be the cause of your destruction? What if that person that you desire more than anything else will be the very one to suffocate the life out of you and make your life a living hell? What if that person brings nothing but harm to you? Yet you sit there wondering why your prayers aren't being answered, when if you look closely, you will see that they are.

Far Away from Pain

One day you will come so far from what you've been through, far, far away from the grief that you thought would never leave you. So be a little more patient, because that day is not too far away *In Sha Allah*.

Past and Future

In a *haraam* relationship a girl worries about her boyfriend's past, and the boyfriend worries about the girlfriend's future. There is never any peace; just anxiety, guilt and worry which worsen once both end up broken.

Qadr

It was Allah's *Qadr*. Let this be your closure.

Laugh

Don't fall for a guy just because he makes you laugh; he could turn out to be the very reason for your endless tears.

Love

Love doesn't leave scars, mistakes do. Don't confuse your first 'love' with your first 'mistake'.

Human Devil

Have you ever met a human devil? They come in beautiful disguises and leave you traumatised, haunted for life.

Move On

You must believe that what happened has happened for the best. You have to believe it was Allah's way of protecting you from harm. So put your trust in Allah and move on.

Option

If you want a man to take you seriously, then you must at first take yourself seriously. Set your standards high; aim to be his wife, and not just an option in his life.

Fear Allah

Dear Brothers, if you do not want anyone to seduce, touch, play, cheat or break your sisters' or mother's hearts, then do not seduce, touch, play, cheat or break other people's sisters' and mothers' hearts. Fear Allah brothers, fear Allah!

Boundaries

"My intentions are pure". But how can you know the intention of the other person? You can't. Keep friendships within the boundaries of Islam - it's the best protection for you.

It's not Love

It's not love, it is simply an addiction. It's so easy to confuse it with love but all it is a figment of your imagination. Your mind knows the truth, as does your heart deep down. Just listen.

Worth

Make your tears count. Don't waste them on people that don't deserve you, on people that Allah removed from your life for a good reason. But make your tears count by crying tears of love and repentance, tears of thankfulness all for Allah. They are the only tears worth shedding.

Courageous

One day I pray that you have the courage to walk away from all the things that are holding you back from living your purpose, from all the things that are silently breaking your heart and taking you away from God. I pray that you courageously walk away from all the things that are hindering you from achieving your greatest self.

Any good is from Allah alone

And

Any mistake is from myself and Shaytaan.

May Allah accept the good from me and you and forgive our mistakes

Aameen.